THE GENERIC DEMANDS
OF GREEK LITERATURE

by

Frederic Will

© Editions Rodopi N.V., Amsterdam 1976
Printed in the Netherlands
ISBN: 90–6203–447–0

For Betty
who is always looking for the real Greece

Acknowledgments

Several of the following essays have been previously published, in somewhat different form: 'Dilemma in Attic Tragedy,' *Edda*, LXVI (1966), 1-11; 'Prometheus and Literary Self-Awareness,' *American Journal of Philology*, LXXXIII (1962), 72-85; 'Transcendent Character in Greek Drama,' *Texas Studies in Language and Literature*, VII (1965), 137-144; 'The Knowing of Greek Tragedy,' *Journal of Aesthetics and Art Criticism*, XVI (1958), 510-518; 'Objectivity in Homer,' *Texas Studies in Language and Literature*, VII (1965), 5-15; 'Hesiod's Transitional Version of Epic Demand' (under different title), *Symbolae Osloenses*, XXXVI (1961), 5-14; 'Solon's Consciousness of Himself,' *Transactions of the American Philological Association*, LXXXIX (1958), 301-311; 'Sappho and Poetic Motion,' *The Classical Journal*, LXVI (1966), 259-262; 'Archilochus and his Senses,' *The Classical Journal*, LVII (1962), 289-296. I am grateful to the editors of those journals for permission to reprint.

CONTENTS

Preface

The following collection consists of nine closely related essays, each of which considers a portion of the work of an ancient Greek author. The method of 'considering' is in almost every case a mixture of explication de texte with cultural history. These analyses have been directed, as far as possible, to a general audience: that is, to a broad spectrum of readers concerned with Western literary history.

A general thread runs through, and binds, the nine essays. That thread is thematic; it develops the conviction that the genres of ancient Greek literature are meaningfully related to one another, and to the works belonging 'categorically' under them. The final argument is that these genre-categories — epic, lyric, and dramatic — were 'demanding' and 'stipulating' factors, as well as 'intelligibility-granting' factors, in the growth of ancient Greek literature.

Most of these essays have been published before — though in a radically different form — as the acknowledgments page will indicate. But it was not until long after writing the essays that I became aware of the generic argument they illustrate. That unexpected becoming-aware is itself relevant here. It followed and illuminated concrete experience of Greek literary texts, in just the way that the genre-categories themselves follow and illuminate the same texts.

Amherst Massachusetts
March, 1973

'All is dispute when one leaves
his own nature
And does things that misfit it.'
(Neoptolemus, in *Philoctetes*)

Chapter I

Dillema in Attic Tragedy

1

The characters of the starker Aeschylean drama — of the *Suppliants*, the *Persians*, the *Seven Against Thebes* — behave like characters in a rite: their movements, speeches and motivations are largely formal, as are those of figures in older Near Eastern work. Pelasgus, Atossa, Eteocles, Prometheus are all poised in the stances of oratorio. This is most obvious, and most worth studying, in the case of Pelasgus, in Aeschylus' *Suppliants.* In introducing himself to the suppliant maidens he gives no hint that he might exist, or know himself, as anything but a 'public existence': like many Homeric heroes he defines himself entirely in terms of his lineage and possessions, digressing at the end only to explain the origin of his city. Yet by the time of his departure (l. 523) from that part of the play, we know he has, in plain view, revealed something of his inwards, has opened himself to us. Dilemma has been the opening wedge.

In a series of speeches (ll. 375-80; 386-91; 397-401; 407-17) Pelasgus shows increasing awareness of the size of his dilemma: the gross apparent necessity of choosing between the maidens and his state. He sizes the dilemma up quickly, putting it gnomically (377-8):

Without
Harm I cannot aid you; nor is it sensible
To despise these your earnest prayers.
(Trans. of *Suppliants* by Benardete)

And he is openly frightened by the problem (379-80):

I am at a loss, and fearful is my heart,
To act or not to act and choose success.

On the whole, though, we are struck by the impersonality of Pelasgus' statement about his emotions. It is almost as if he were talking about another person: we hear little of the anguish, yet, of Agamem-

non's (in *Iphigeneia at Aulis*) 'What shall I do . . .?' We also notice
the official depersonalizing insistence that the whole matter must be
referred to the people ('I share with all the citizens,') (369),
('. . . never would I act alone, apart from the people . . .') (398-9).
This insistence is quite in character for the ruler; but it is significant
that Aeschylus chose to work with a character for whom such
behavior would be appropriate. As a man of state, Pelasgus turns
readily to formalities which cloak, and seem almost to become, his
feelings.

We feel closer to Pelasgus' personal involvement when he
imagines how the people might blame him if his judgment proves
wrong. Already the details of his dilemma are growing clearer to him.
He imagines his people saying (401):

'Respecting aliens the city you destroyed.'

In telling a second person (the chorus) how a third speaker might
address him, Pelasgus takes us farther into his mood, imagining
himself involved in a context, as a center of interest. The unbroken
surface of his address to the chorus seems temporarily disturbed. In
his last speech to the chorus (407-17), before he retires to meditate,
he does something with this revelation of his inner existence, lets
what he is express itself with a new freedom. Moving onto the level
of literary imagery, he compares thought (*phrontis*) to a diver
(*kolumbeter*) who must descend deeply into the depths, watching
carefully. In itself this comparison, full of sensuous images, is a new
invitation to the chorus to feel with Pelasgus, to sympathize with his
point-of-view. This particular image, involving a descent into the
depths of the mind, is an especially forceful way of dramatizing for
the chorus the kind of inner descent which the king finds himself
obliged to make.

Before his later re-entrance (438) then, we are better acquainted with Pelasgus, to some extent because he – compelled by
the concern of his dilemma – has been acquainting us with himself.
After re-entering he expatiates, in his two main speeches (437-54;
468-89), on the problem at hand. By now his sense of the danger of
the situation has grown more vivid. He gives it its strongest formulation (442):

. . . yet anchorage is never
Free from pain.

He is terribly shocked to hear the girls' suicide threat, which makes the 'physical' menace of the situation newly fresh to him 'Whip to the heart,' he calls it (466). Once again he opens to us. In the speech (468-80) following that suicide threat he dramatizes his feeling of fear, which above he had only named (379). The whole problem has worn him out: 'Alas! everywhere I'm gripped in strangleholds . . .' (468). He accentuates his feeling through imagery, by which we are brought into closer and more intimate touch (469-71):

> and like a swollen river evils flood:
> Embarked on a sea of doom uncrossed, abysmal,
> Nowhere is anchorage.

While shortly before (438-441) he had said:

> I have pondered, and here I'm run aground:
> Gainst you or them necessity is strained
> For mighty way as fastly drawn as ships
> Held by the windlass: . . .

Perhaps this metaphor may seem too baroque to be a direct expression of inner nature. Even more than before (407 ff.) however, we feel drawn into sympathy with the speaker's sensuous vision. The tenseness of his inner situation is vividly suggested by the verb 'to draw, or strain,' (*gegomphotai*). His earlier self-introduction, and his rational declarations about dilemma and responsibilities, did not express a deep, or 'intimate', center of the king's being. He had seemed to be working off the formal surface of his being. In fact Pelasgus' dilemma has hardly been with him long enough, at this point, to work its way deeply into his feelings. In metaphorical expressions of anxiety he brings us much closer to himself. The same kind of deepening awareness, in him, may be felt in his increasing friendliness toward the maidens, a friendliness he expresses in his last major speech. Here – in contrast to the prudent distance which he had previously kept – he shows himself ready to help. He advises the girls to move their suppliant boughs to a more conspicuous altar (481-85), so that their arrival will be well known. And for the first time he explicitly sides with the girls' position, advising them to move their boughs in order that (187-88):

> Pity they (the townspeople) may feel
> For you, and hate those men's arrogance.

Pelasgus' open adoption of this position is new, and lets us see that he *has* been thinking, deepening his opinion, in the course of the preceding dialogue. Tacitly, but powerfully, his new behavior strikes at us. Of course we have been prepared, by his statement (478-79) that Zeus, the protector of suppliants, must be honored. But what we find, in the present friendliness of Pelasgus, is more than an expression of religious orthodoxy. It is an internally motivated change of heart, the king's most significant self-revelation as a character with an inner life, with a 'private', as distinct from a 'public,' existence. (In that respect it is like the moment in *Gilgamesh* when Gilgamesh realizes that Enkidu is dead.) Final evidence of the reality of Pelasgus' change comes a few lines later (517-19), when he reassures the girls: 'I shall go and call my citizens together,' he says, 'that I may make them well-disposed toward you. And I will teach your father to say such things' (that is, as will make the people well-disposed). All his earlier insistence on turning the matter over to the people has been forgotten. He has taken a firm position within his dilemma, has even, in a sense, passed through and transcended it. We feel sure that he cannot turn back now, and we are confirmed by his later (949 ff.), vigorous defense of the girls against the Egyptians.

ii

The dilemma facing Neoptolemus (in Sophocles' *Philoctetes*) is harder to formulate than that of Pelasgus. The latter was torn between the claims of the girls and those of easy safety for his state. Neoptolemus is exposed to a dilemma but he is not torn between two apparently valid directions of action; from the beginning we guess that he will never accept Odysseus' unscrupulousness, will never be crucially tempted by that position. (With Pelasgus we were in genuine doubt. He could have gone in either direction). Neoptolemus is concerned to know *how* to help Philoctetes, how to be himself, and in a sense to know whether he has the courage to be himself. This final doubt — whether he can be himself — is as close as we can come to formulating his dilemma, which in this sense resembles Hamlet's dilemma. In other words Neoptolemus' dilemma is already more nebulous — as Sophocles handles it — than the dilemma of Pelasgus.

Accordingly there is no rapid decisiveness required of, or found in, Neoptolemus, as there is in Pelagus. Yet Neoptolemus, too, is forced by dilemma into an increasingly intimate self-revelation. It is less a revelation of different facets, or traits, of his nature than it is of the same basic nature — the idealistic young man — under the stress of different forms of *Machtpolitik.* Dilemma simply opens him up.

His recognition of dilemma is apparent in those lines (86-95) in which he reacts to Odysseus' plan for the taking of the bow. The formality with which Neoptolemus expresses his outrage is comparable to the formality of Pelasgus, when he introduces himself to the suppliants. In Neoptolemus, though, we see this difference; that he is defining himself not in terms of anything external – his possession, or lineage – but in terms of his *ethos,* the mode of being habitual to him, through which he has acquired something of a 'generally' human personality. When he says (86-87):

> 'Son of Laertes, what I dislike to hear
> I hate to put in execution,'
> (Trans. of *Philoctetes* by David Grene)

we feel that he is acting a part, being 'typical,' although his following remarks qualify our impression, making it clear for example that while Neoptolemus hates guile, he is willing to use force on Philoctetes.

When we next see Neoptolemus in the grips of his dilemma we suddenly touch him more closely, as though we hadn't really known him before. In a long, lying speech to Philoctetes (343-90), Neoptolemus had intentionally concealed himself, and had seemed to acquiesce in that corrupting strategy proposed by Odysseus at the start of the play. However when Philoctetes is first attacked with his illness (732 ff.) a situation begins to announce itself in which Neoptolemus can harvest the fruit of deceit, and steal the bow. He confesses to the chorus (839-42) that he knows the time has come to strike and steal. Yet he does nothing while Philoctetes is sleeping, during which time – the choral passage (843-64) – we imagine Neoptolemus tortured with indecision. (His gestures, on stage, would be reinforcing this sense of agony.) When Philoctetes wakes up Neoptolemus seems delighted, thinking he will now be freed of his anguish. But this relief is short-lived, because Neoptolemus' scruples overcome him. His dilemma floods back. To it we owe his remarkable, irrepressible overflowings of inner struggle: a pair of lines (895 and 897) which baffle the evidently unsuspecting Philoctetes. Neoptolemus says:

> Now is the moment, what shall I do from now on?

and

I do not know what to say. I am at a loss.

Challenged to explain his outburst he offers a generalization — which now has much more poignancy than his philosophical statements to Odysseus, at the outset of the play. Now he says (902-3):

> All is disgust when one leaves his own nature
> and does things that misfit it

Nowhere else does he grasp and express his dilemma as well as here, where we feel in the presence, summoned by the play's advance, of a hard-won inner truth. It is no surprise when, shortly after (915-16), inner pressure obliges Neoptolemus to tell Philoctetes the truth. That pressure is almost 'physically' apparent to us in Neoptolemus' words.

Neoptolemus' honesty reflects no decisive change or permanent determination. At the entrance of Odysseus (977) the atmosphere of still-possible compromise between Philoctetes and Neoptolemus is polluted, and Neoptolemus himself vanishes temporarily from the scene, suppressed and frustrated in his good intentions, his dilemma unsolved. It is not until line 1224 that we see him return, with Odysseus, determined to reaffirm his sympathy for Philoctetes:

> I go to undo the wrong that I have done.

In the ensuing wrangle between Neoptolemus and Odysseus, we can imagine ourselves again at the opening of the play, when Neoptolemus first bridled at Odysseus' suggestions. No real change has occurred in either man's stance: the younger man seems to have moved back and forth through his dilemma, with a clearly dramatized pendulous motion. Shortly, however, he reveals the surprising way in which he has been acquiring the momentum necessary to action, a new action which will break forth from indecision. (Here, as with Gilgamesh or Pelasgus, the gradual *deepening* of character is nicely, and suddenly, revealed to us). Almost without realizing it we have been prepared for Neoptolemus' defiance toward Odysseus, his turning-over of the bow to Philoctetes. In a sense, this act might be considered the solution to the younger man's dilemma; but it is not that decisive a move, does not have the finality of Pelasgus' decision to shelter the suppliants. The *status quo* of Neoptolemus' conscience has simply been restored by the returning of the bow. After the troubled history of his good intentions, in this play, he cannot feel complacent or final about this last virtue of action. He is still loyal enough to Odysseus, whom he will prevent Philoctetes from shooting; while his desire for unity, and for the harmonious conclusion which only Heracles can introduce into the play, is frustrated by the continuing refusal of Philoctetes to return to Troy. Neoptolemus himself, then, moves in this play through a dilemma which is not really soluble, both because he is not sufficiently determined, and because conditions external to him — such as the attitude of Philoctetes — refuse to seal his situation with a harmonious conclusion. But we become well acquainted with him, in his indecisiveness. Dilemma has revealed him to us.

iii

Agamemnon (in Euripides' *Iphigeneia at Aulis*) reveals himself, like Neoptolemus, only gradually through his dilemma: also like Neoptolemus, he is faced with an imprecisely definable dilemma, not with the kind of either-or crisis which faced Pelasgus.

From the start of the *Iphigeneia at Aulis* we sense that Agamemnon will follow the order of Calchas, and have Iphigeneia sacrificed. Paternal and conscientious Agamemnon may be, but he is foremost a public man, putting state responsibilities first. Like Neoptolemus', his dilemma concerns not so much what he should do, but whether he can do it, and how he should do it: how he should handle Clytemnestra; what he can say to Iphigeneia. To such questions, self-addressed under the stress of crisis, Agamemnon can naturally offer no clear-cut answers. He can simply reveal himself in a number of changing foci, until Euripides has lighted up the maximum of humanity in him.

By skillful use of the faithful old manservant, Euripides makes the tortured Agamemnon reveal himself, at the beginning of the play, with an intimacy which is rare in Greek tragedy. None of the characters mentioned earlier, here, is opened so far as this. The scene before Agamemnon's tent is unusually secluded, close to nature — we are keenly aware of the stars — and still. The King says (9-11):

> No voice is there of birds even,
> Or of the sea's waves.
> The silence of the winds
> Holds hushed the river.
> (Trans. of *Iphigeneia* by Charles Walker).

In this context we feel Agamemnon's inner existence peculiarly ready to be disclosed. His anguish of dilemma is revealed by the old man in acute, physically precise lines (34-40):

But you've lit your lamp and
Been writing a letter, haven't you?
You still have it in your hand —
With those same words you've
Been putting together. You seal
The letter up — and then tear
The seal open. You've been doing it
Over and over again. Then you
Throw the torch on the ground,
And bulging tears come down out
Of your eyes . . .

As often, Euripides uses a second person to bring out the feelings of a main character. (In this way Agamemnon's dilemma is made more tangible and intimate than those of Pelasgus or Neoptolemus). Agamemnon himself shows the anguish of his position, shortly after, by rather incoherently muttering the contents of his letter (119-23). He is thoroughly distracted. Just before sending the old man off to Clytemnestra, with the letter urging Iphigeneia not to be sent, he cries out (136-37):

My mind is crazed, I fall in ruin!

Sending this letter seems so improper to Agamemnon, that he feels almost divinely guilty, struck by divine wrath. We sense that he will not be able to evade his public duty, and that his vacillation will doom him. But his dilemma is not to be so easily solved, because its solution lies outside him.

He further shows the quality of his sensitivity when (440-63) he confronts Menelaus, after their quarrel and the announcement of Clytemnestra's arrival. Agamemnon's distress drives him even to a reconciliation with his brother. He seems relieved at his brother's interception of the letter — since he is no longer obliged to ignore his public duty. Between themselves the rulers feelingly discuss the problems of the great. Yet though safely isolated now, in the domain of public responsibility, Agamemnon shows himself capable of an extraordinarily fine projection into his family's viewpoints. Dilemma hones his feelings to a pure articulateness. Much as he regrets his wife's coming he admits that it is only natural (457-59):

. . . coming she only obeys nature,
Following a daughter here to do love's services,
And give the bride away.

Then he puts words into Iphigeneia's mouth, and imagines her saying
(463-64):

> O Father, why do you kill me? May Death
> Be your bride also and betroth
> All of your dear ones as he has plighted me!

Here Agamemnon has given up any serious effort to save his daughter, and is humble to what he knows is fated for him, imagining a real, and inevitable, crisis. He spares himself nothing. He even imagines the infant Orestes' cries (465-66):

> The infant will cry out
> Meaningless words, but full of meaning
> To my heart!

Agamemnon could hardly go beyond this, in facing the poignancy of his situation. Yet even here he is not concerned with *whether* to sacrifice Iphigeneia, only with what attitude to adopt toward, with what courage to meet, the inevitability of that sacrifice. The persistent intangibility of his problem follows him.

His final statement of decision is made to both his wife and his daughter. After wretched subterfuges, and humiliating efforts to deceive his wife, the king reaches a kind of plateau. His attitude is stronger, and diminishingly poignant. He does still say (1255-56):

> My daughter and wife, I know what calls
> To me for pity and compassion, and
> What does not.

But now his tone is less passionate, and more determined. Throughout his address — for this time he seems to speak as a man of state — he emphasizes the *external* compulsion under which he acts (1269-72):

> Nor am I here
> At Menelaus' will, but Greece lays upon me
> This sacrifice of you beyond a will
> Of mine. We are weak and of no account
> Before this fated thing.

Agamemnon seems to have solved his dilemma, adopting a freeing attitude. Yet like Neoptolemus and unlike Pelasgus, he is trapped in a dilemma for which there is no precise solution. To solve his dilemma Agamemnon must rely on the impersonal, on external compulsion. He himself cannot be the solver. To that degree we feel his insecurity even at the end. He has chosen to let fate spare him from himself. But this impression cannot hide the wretchedness of his spirit, which has been opened forth.

iv

The presentation of dilemma is one important means toward the revelation of characters' inner life in ancient Greek tragedy. There is no reason, though, to overstate the importance of dilemma in Greek tragedy, where few characters are found in whom 'the native hue of resolution is sicklied o'er with the pale cast of thought.' Furthermore there are a good many characters in Greek tragedy — Clytemnestra, Antigone, Creon, Medea — in whom deep self-revelation is achieved without the help of any such dramatic device. Pelasgus' dilemma appears to be one of tragedy's most important early breakthroughs into inner existence. It is a literary event. In the wake of it many further characters struggle with dilemma: we can think of them as indebted to plays like the *Suppliants,* and to *its* doubtless numerous predecessors, for part of their own depth. The tradition they form is a limited one. But it is profound, and full of its own future.

'You see before you him that gave
fire to men
even Prometheus.'
(Prometheus, in *Prometheus Bound*)

Chapter II

Prometheus and Literary Self-Awareness

i

Aeschylus grasped his Prometheus deeply and from the inside. Later literature testifies to the importance of the character Prometheus, by elaborating endlessly on the Prometheian theme, making that character now a defender of eternally worthy humanity, now an incarnation of the folly of attempting to help man against God's will now a living proof of the hostility of divinity toward man.[1] I believe we are dealing, here, with a character of more symbolic pregnance than the three discussed in the first chapter. In the course of our dealings, though, we will find ourselves taken directly back into that chapter.

Kitto, in his *Greek Tragedy,* offers the idea that Aeschylus' characters – he is thinking especially of Agamemnon and Xerxes – are simply personified *hybris*: 'it (*hybris*) is something without which these heroes would not exist; it is all of them that matters.'[2] This is too simple. Kitto's remarks on Prometheus are more complex but still shelter difficulties. Kitto thinks that *hybris* is prominent in Prometheus, and that it consists of stubbornness, a stubborn pride. He is careful to distinguish this pride from *hamartia,* at least in

1. H. W. Smyth, *Aeschylean Tragedy* (Berkeley, 1924), 92-7, remarks, with good analyses, on the most important literary works based on the Prometheus-theme. At least one work of genuine interest, published since Smyth, should be mentioned: E. A. Havelock's *The Crucifixion of Intellectual Man* (Boston, 1951), a reworking of the *Prometheus Bound* in which Zeus is taken as the eternal bureaucrat, Prometheus as the progressive scientist seeking to cast new light.
2. H. D. F. Kitto, *Greek Tragedy* (New York, 1954), 117. Kitto's view of Prometheus must be read out of two sections of his book: p. 111, where he considers, in general, the one-trait nature of the Aeschylean hero; p. 117, where he remarks on Prometheus as a character.

Aristotle's sense, since it is clear that pride is not an 'error' in judgment through which Prometheus has fallen.

Stubborn pride, in the *Prometheus Bound,* seems to Kitto to be the chief trait of Prometheus, a trait placed – in Aeschylus' way – conspicuously in the foreground of the play. Kitto alludes to other 'traits,' especially to philanthropy, but only in passing.

Max Pohlenz, in *Die griechische Tragödie,* develops an equally definite notion of the character of Prometheus. Like Kitto he emphasizes the lack of complex, vital selfhood in Prometheus: "Nicht vom Charakter und vom Innenleben der Person aus hat der Dichter das Drama gestaltet' (p. 81). ('The poet did not work out from character and inner life in shaping the drama.')[3] Pohlenz thinks character in general is of interest to Aeschylus only as a contribution to the *Handlung* represented in the drama. Putting his own point negatively, he is ready to see in Prometheus a development – almost an outcropping – required by the plot of the *Prometheus Bound.* On this theory Prometheus would not be quite an allegorical figure, primarily meaningful through references which transcended his play. He would, however, share with the allegorical figures a lack of distinct personality.

Common to these, and to most, theories about the *Prometheus Bound* is the view that Prometheus is no realistic, lifelike organic character. But there is something wrong with the view. I wonder whether Prometheus does not show and *vitally embody* a number of significant traits. In the *Prometheus Bound,* where the character's stubbornness is obviously called for, we still see him in less grand moods, displaying humbler traits which are organic to him. In his first two interchanges with the chorus (136-44; 152-9)[4] he clearly asks for sympathy; his awful isolation has just become clear to him, and he needs to be consoled. And later, describing the benefits which he has brought to men (445-68; 478-506), he expresses that stirring philanthropy which has endeared him to mortals. In both moods this character shows himself as more complex than an incarnation of stubborn pride. His traits seem to be vitally unified,

---

3. Max Pohlenz, *Die griechische Tragödie* (Göttingen, 1954). Cf., for an overall appreciation of Pohlenz's – and other significant German scholars' – conceptions of "character" in Greek tragedy, W. Zürcher, *Die Darstellung des Menschen im Drama des Euripides* (Basel, 1947).

4. All line references are to Gilbert Murray's text (Oxford, 1937).

not just to be signs which he puts up to indicate which mood is on top at a given time. His pride implies his philanthropy: he is not proud for no reason, but because he has given enormous gifts to man. His pride is involved with his 'weakness,' his wish for sympathy: that weakness is the single sign of strain which makes Prometheus' pride real and convincing. We can ask Pohlenz whether the character of Prometheus doesn't also have an inner unity, a nature which binds together his different traits. Otherwise, how could they seem to be vitally interwoven? We can ask about that unity, which Pohlenz dismisses by claiming that Prometheus is essentially organized from 'without,' from the plot. In doing this we also help ourselves to understand more about that tradition of characterization in which Aeschylus was writing. This understanding will throw light back into the problems of the first chapter.

To the extent that there is a direction of movement in the *Prometheus Bound* it converges exclusively on Prometheus. It has been written, with various ingenious elaborations, that the lesser characters of the play contribute to, or simply 'bring out,' the central character.[5] Zeus himself exists for us here only as a preoccupation of Prometheus. The drama in the mind of the unmoving Titan is seen as the only true movement in the play. Not only does all the action of the play revolve about, and converge on, the main character, but all that impinges on Prometheus is drawn into the core of his inner awareness of himself, made one in himself. Such self-awareness is the unifying principle in Prometheus. One of the clearest examples of it is his awareness of his 'convictions,' of the intellectual position which he occupies and is. This aspect of his awareness can be isolated by observing Prometheus' responses to new characters who come on stage.

5. One of the most helpful expressions of this idea can be found in Gilbert Norwood, *Greek Tragedy* (London, 1948), 96: "All the secondary characters act as a foil to bring the central figure into massive relief. Each has some touch of Prometheus: Hephaestus, pity without self-sacrifice; Cratos, strength without reflection; the Nymphs, tenderness without force; Oceanus, common-sense without dignity; Io, sensibility to suffering without the vision which learns the lesson of pain; Hermes, the power to serve without perception of the secret of sovereignty." E. T. Owen, in *The Harmony of Aeschylus* (Toronto, 1952), 58, writes: "All of them (Hephaestus, Oceanus, Io) are at heart in sympathy with Prometheus; what they don't approve of is his self-chosen suffering."

He faintly senses the first entrance of the chorus; then immediately we hear his (119-23):

> You see me a wretched God in chains,
> the enemy of Zeus, hated of all
> the Gods that enter Zeus' palace hall,
> because of my excessive love for Man.
> (Trans. *of Prometheus Bound* by David Grene).

The last line is a leitmotif of Prometheus' self-awareness and to it he constantly relates his experiences. When Oceanus appears, Prometheus is first extremely sensitive to the appearance he himself makes, then promptly identifies himself in terms of his convictions (304-5):

> Now look and see
> the sight, this friend of Zeus, that helped set up
> his tyranny and see what agonies
> twist me, by his instructions!

Understandably enough, he does not for a moment forget who he is; more important, he never fails to remind his interlocutors of what he has stood for. This obsession is clearest at the entrance of Io. In his first words (589-90) he simply takes startled cognizance of her arrival;[6] but as soon as she has identified herself further he promises (609-11) to tell her what she wants to know; and identifies himself (612) by:

> You see before you him that gave fire to men,
> even Prometheus.

During each of these entrances of lesser characters Prometheus promptly identifies himself, referring to the 'position' he has occupied through actions and through continuing conviction. He is presently this position, and the persistent awareness of it is one form of his self-awareness.

The unity of his character can be introduced through this matter of his position. He refers continually to it. Furthermore, his constant inner awareness of his convictions is consequential for the play. For in such terms the play is rendered until the end entirely

---

6. The extreme, emotional responsiveness of Prometheus to new beings who enter his sense-field can be understood in terms of the place of "fear" and "anguish" in Aeschylus. For an excellent treatment of that question, cf. Jacqueline de Romilly, *La crainte et l'angoisse dans le théâtre d'Eschyle* (Paris, 1958).

uneventful. So far from its being true, as Pohlenz argues, that Prometheus' character is formed 'vom aussen,' that character is impregnable 'vom aussen.' In a sense, nothing except a natural catastrophe *can* happen to Prometheus. The Prometheus of the *Prometheus Bound* could not change, for he turns about the *idée fixe* of his convictions. In this he differs from all the dilemma-tugged, thus off-balance, characters considered earlier.

Prometheus' awareness of having been wronged for his position is a function of his awareness of himself as a position. This mode of inner awareness adds a depth and point to his sense of position which, in itself, could become simply a tiresomely repeated motif. We are, as it happens, continually driven to experience his awareness of having been victimized.

Frequently — in six important passages,[7] he draws attention to this injustice. The unsolicited quality of the first instance (107-8; 112-13), while Prometheus is still alone and unaware of the arriving nymphs, alerts us to the interiority of his sense of injustice. Apparently addressing the audience, but really only himself, he says (107-8):

> It was a mortal man
> to whom I gave great privileges and
> for that was yoked in this unyielding harness.

Then, after mentioning his gifts of fire to mortals, and the benefit thus conferred, he adds (112-13):

> This is the sin committed
> for which I stand accountant, and I pay
> Nailed in my chains under the open sky.

The other examples of inwardly protest follow either of two directions: they repeat this complaint, that Prometheus' service to mankind has been badly repaid by Zeus; or claim that Prometheus' services to Zeus have been badly repaid. In either case the blame falls on Zeus, who as main object of reproach temporarily preoccupies consciousness. After having described to the chorus (199-221) his original efforts to help the Titans. then his decision to help Zeus, and the great assistance he provided to Zeus, he says (221-3):

> These were the services
> I rendered to this tyrant and these pains
> the payment he has given me in requital.

7. *Prometheus Bound*, 112 -13, 221 -3, 239 -41, 268 -70, 305 -6, 469 -71.

Or somewhat later he exclaims, also to the chorus (267):

In helping Man I brought my troubles on me.

When not much farther (304-6), we meet the lines,

Now look and see
the sight, this friend of Zeus, that helped set up
his tyranny and see what agonies
twist me, by his instruction!

we see how formulaic, and part of a distinctive pattern of self-awareness, this response is in him. We touch lightly here, perhaps, on the paradox of his character: that he is both introspective and without distinct, 'human' personality. Again, he differs from any figure studied earlier; he is more diaphanous and abstract.

Prometheus has a continually dramatized sense of himself as powerful, as, in addition to occupying a distinct position for which he has been wronged, being a secret-holder. He makes at least ten[8] important allusions to his secret — the knowledge of how Zeus will be deposed. Though these allusions play an obvious 'external' part in the structure of the play, as the only evidence we have of Prometheus' real power, they acquire — for reasons inherent to the nature of secrecy — a dramatic quality which is more deeply relevant. By awareness of what he knows, and what no one else in the play knows, Prometheus is made supremely conscious of his own distinctness and individual separateness. As a secret-holder he is identical with the Prometheus who is aware of his convictions, and with the Prometheus who feels mistreated; they are all modes of a single recurrent introspection.[9] The holding of a secret, furthermore, gives

8. *Prometheus Bound*, 169-71, 189, 520, 756, 870-4, 908-10, 913-15, 939-40, 963, 996-7.

9. For the character of Prometheus to reach this stage of reflective refinement, much "purifying" of earlier forms of the myth — as Hesiod preserves them, for instance — had to take place. Gilbert Murray discusses that process of refinement well in his *Aeschylus, the Creator of Tragedy* (Oxford, 1940), 21-32. A suitable awareness of the "inwardly" quality of Prometheus, however, is hard to find. Rarely, in more recent writings, does one find remarks as sensible and perceptive as those of Maurice Croiset, who wrote in his *Histoire de la littérature grecque* (Paris, 1913), III, 214: "Comme le poète qui les a créés, ils (the characters of Aeschylus) sont tous méditatifs. Leur pensée dominante les obsède et repasse sans cesse dans leur esprit sous de nouvelles formes"; while if one wishes to chart the entire development of self-consciousness in Greek

to Prometheus' introspections a potency which enriches their unity
A consideration of Prometheus' 'traits' has meaning only in terms of
this richly unified form of existence. Those traits have no existence
in isolation.

I could further analyze Prometheus' central, unifying inner
awareness. I could pay attention to his felt and expressed sense of
being immortal, an important ingredient, like the secret itself, in our

Geistesgeschichte – an undertaking relevant to the problem at hand in this
Chapter – he is helped little by available scholarship. Bruno Snell's *The Discovery of The Mind,* trans. Rosenmeyer (Cambridge, Mass., 1953), is one great help;
and there are especially valuable suggestions, among the literature known to me,
in E. Petersen, *Die attische Tragödie* (Bonn, 1915); Hermann Fränkel, *Dichtung
und Philosophie des frühen Griechentums* (New York, 1951); W. Zürcher
(above, note 3); Eliza Wilkins, *The Delphic Maxims in Literature* (Chicago,
1929). Doubtless further valuable suggestions, from the viewpoint of the
classical philologist, may be found. Yet to take advantage of presently available
help, with this problem in Geistesgeschichte, one must promptly call other
branches of inquiry to his aid. From available philosophical, psychoanalytical,
and sociological works, the overall historical picture can be at least imagined. J.
Beare, in his *Greek Theories of Elementary Cognition* (Oxford, 1906), finds,
even in Aristotle – and less in other writers – little deep interest in consciousness or the self. He writes: "In spite of the importance assigned to consciousness
in the *Nicomachean Ethics,* it remains in general for Aristotle a psychical
παρεργον, utterly without the importance assigned to it by modern psycholo-
gists" (p. 290). Our suspicion that the search for deep introspection was a long
and slow one among the Greeks may be clarified by such a book as Geza
Roheim's *The Origin and Function of Culture* (New York, 1943); that book,
illustrating the thesis that the development of culture is an accommodation to
the long, dependent, infantile stage of man, points out both man's natural
resistance to true independence, and self-understanding, and the gradual
assistance of culture in overcoming that resistance. Finally, if we wish to observe
our question from a sociological-historical standpoint, we might begin by con-
sulting such general works as Samuel Noah Kramer, *From the Tablets of Sumer*
(Indian Hills, Colorado, 1956); John Wilson, *The Burden of Egypt* (Chicago,
1951); or George Thomson, *Studies in Ancient Greek Society: The Prehistoric
Aegean* (New York, 1949). From the consideration of such works we might
form a clearer sense of the long struggle toward a sense of the individual, and
toward the individual's sense of himself, in early Mediterranean culture. The
establishment of such broad contexts is peculiarly useful for the understanding
of the growth of self-awareness in, say, Greek tragedy: the immediate Hellenic
evidence is scarce, and there is significant continuity between Greek and earlier
Near-Eastern cultures.

experience of his situation. Then there is evidently deep fear of appearing ludicrous. In any such extension of argument we would be probing deeper into the character than we could through the language of 'traits.' But the point must not be overdone. We cannot properly speak of Prometheus as 'self-conscious.' We don't read the play as though he – even to the extent of Oedipus or Phaedra, and certainly not to that of Gilgamesh or Neoptolemus – has a self which he is searching for. In fact, Prometheus is simply a living awareness of the contents of his consciousness, of such preoccupations as what he stands for, how he has been mistreated, what potent knowledge he possesses. He further distinguishes himself from such a character as Oedipus by being nothing but such inner awareness. By being so, Prometheus lives his various traits – pride, philanthropy, even softness – in the vitally unified way in which he himself exists.

ii

The kind of inner awareness we find in the character of Prometheus has interesting parallels to, and can be usefully distinguished from, the handling in other plays of Aeschylus.

The suppliant maidens, as I at least suggested in the first chapter, are inwardly aware, and are so in a way which reminds us of Prometheus. They lack distinctive 'personality,' as is natural in a group of fifty choral members. Yet they can be seen as the chief 'character' of their play, attracting, as they do, more attention even than Pelasgus. They concern us chiefly through their fear. Though in one sense that fear is caused by onrushing Egyptian cousins, it is in fact largely interiorized in the play, and transformed into the object of an inner obsession. Appropriately enough, given their helplessness, the girls are entirely the victims of their inner emotional life (while Pelasgus was the victim of his dilemma). The awareness of the contents of their consciousness is in this play virtually all that the girls are, and in this mode of being they resemble Prometheus. When the herald of the Egyptians first appears (825) we are shocked by the intrusion of the genuinely external.[10]

The difference between the central introspection of this play and that of *Prometheus Bound* is also interesting. The suppliants

10. Another aspect of the "internal" dimension of this play has been excellently analyzed by Snell (above, note 9, p. 102), who points out that in Pelasgus' struggle of conscience – torn between his own state and the rights of

have a far less differentiated consciousness of which to be aware than Prometheus has. Not only are they self-aware in an exclusively 'affective' way, but their feeling of their own existence is un-rational, and without distinctions. They know themselves as panic; while Prometheus knows himself in terms of rational convictions and of his own powerful secret. This distinctive introspection of the tragic chorus reminds us of its relative proximity to the early Dionysus-chorus, from which tragedy grew. A simple passionate, 'religious' introspection marked off the performances of those rural choruses.

On the point at issue there is also in the *Persians* a relation to, and a distinction from, the *Prometheus Bound*. Again in the *Persians* no single character predominates. The play bathes in a single mood of doom, of which the characters — Darius, the chorus, Xerxes, even Atossa — are vehicles varying from one another only by embodying more or less typical roles: the chorus are miserable elders; Xerxes, the ruined king; Atossa, the articulate but despairing queen, to be met later in the Euripidean Hecuba and Andromache. The single mood reflected by all these characters is itself inwardly, reflected in consciousnesses which are without exception turned in on a central preoccupation, the fate of the Persian forces. As in the *Prometheus Bound* there is a massive, impregnable introspection which no events of the play can quite penetrate. The entrance of Xerxes at the end of the *Persians* only confirms and strengthens the established mood, as the entrance of Hermes can, and does, have no effect on the un-shakeable mood of Prometheus. Yet in the *Persians,* as in the *Suppliants,* there is a firm difference from the *Prometheus Bound.* The introspection is far simpler: its contents are single, deeply felt and undeveloped. We seem closer in mood — if not in time — to the simpler archaic world in which the dilemmas discussed in chapter one deployed themselves.

suppliants — a remarkably deep state of self-awareness is dramatized. This passage from conscience to self-consciousness is also, Snell believes, illustrated by the fragments of Aeschylus' *Myrmidons,* in which Achilles is seen overcoming his own mood, and determining to fight for his men.

'. . . only the king, his hands
before his face,
Shading his eyes as if from
something awful,
Fearful and unendurable to see.'
(Messenger in *Oedipus at Colonus*)

Chapter III

Transcendent Character in Greek Drama

i

The 'transcendent' hero is rare in Greek tragedy, far rarer than dilemma-ridden or introspective characters. It is widely realized — even axiomatic — that the fifth-century Greeks disliked the indefinite, the nebulous, the mysterious, and the infinite. They had no such dislike of dilemma or introspection.

We have found very little of the mysterious or infinite, I think, in the literary works discussed up to this point. The visual art of this entire period offers supporting evidence. Fifth-century Greek sculpture and architecture are marked by a care for definition and clear outline. I am thinking here of the Aegina sculptures, the Apolline figures from Olympia, or of the Parthenon and its sculpture. These creations spring from, and awaken, no haziness, few marginal boundaries of experience. It is true, of course, that we now see these works only without their paint, and outside a living context. But these are relatively superficial elements of the works. Greek drama, considered from the 'formal' viewpoint, is as carefully delimited as are the Greek visual arts: that drama is metrically disciplined; structurally, in its ordering of events, it follows a precise and discernible (though always 'deep') sequence. Even classical Greek philosophy follows this kind of pattern. Xenophanes and Anaxagoras were eager to reduce reality to a single, definable, intelligible principle. The Sophists, for all their casuistry, were obsessed by the idea of clear and distinct thoughts, 'idées claires et distinctes.' It is not that any of these thinkers or artists were 'rationalists,' in the sense which modern philosophy has given that word. Nietzsche, Burckhardt, Fustel de Coulanges, the Cambridge anthropologists, and many others, have educated us on that matter; we are at last beginning to believe that the Greeks were real. We know that we confront in them a culture which was even more tradition-bound, and in ways more shallowly emotional, than ours. But we also know that in its major projections of art and thought it demanded and realized a version of clarity which we have never reached.

In this light we can appreciate the paucity of characters, in classical Greek literature, who extend our understanding to the uncomfortable realms beyond even deep reason. We were not extended in that direction by the experience of Pelasgus, Neoptolemus, or even of Prometheus. Those characters all asked something else from us. This is surprising, for much is said in Greek tragedy about 'recognition' and 'self-knowledge' through tragic suffering. Such statements might make us suppose that the tragic hero regularly passes in his play into the existentially demanding, beyond the limits of ordinary understanding; as if in such cases we were observing, before our own eyes, a growth of religious understanding; were seeing, for instance, a man coming to an essentially new spiritual realization. Still the greatest characters of tragedy – Prometheus, Orestes, Philoctetes, Medea, Heracles – do not seem to pass from us, out of the condition of usual understanding, into conditions which founder our reason. We understand these creations imperfectly, and according to our usually inferior and uninformed powers, but this is because of the depth and wisdom of their creators' work and the temporal distance separating us from them; it is not because of a mystery inherent in the characters and dramatized into their experience. In contrast to these characters, Oedipus at Colonus and Dionysus in the *Bacchae,* transcend *all* familiar experience. They seem to strike out *beyond* the world of Hellenic experience. They drive our experience much farther out than the characters discussed in the last two chapters.

Oedipus, if not more mysterious, is certainly more puzzling to us than he can possibly have been to fifth-century Athenians. Christian and Buddhist wise men are usually supposed to have passed beyond contention and anguish into a condition of spiritual calm. The Buddha went that far; so did Saint Francis and the hermits of the desert. So in fact did Socrates, who meditated to the end over the motives of his behavior, out of a conviction of the validity of calm reason. All these figures have conditioned our conception of the sage. Coming from our great and special distance we too easily judge the 'translated' Oedipus of Colonus by this saintly tradition; we are shocked at his testy behavior in the drama in which he is 'taken up to heaven.' Although by the end of the play Oedipus shows marks of divine favor, for the first three-quarters he is crabby and secular-minded. The only intimation of immortality is his appearance; appropriately ragged, tired, moneyless, and physically maimed. We hear him rant when Ismene, who has just arrived in search of her father, reports that her two brothers could not come to help their father. He exclaims (337-343):

> Ah! They behave as if they were Egyptians,
> Bred the Egyptian way! Down there, the men
> Sit indoors all day long, weaving;
> The women go out and attend to business.
> Just so your brothers, who should have done this work,
> Sit by the fire like home-loving girls,
> And you two, in their place, must bear my hardships.
> (Trans. of *Oedipus at Colonus* by Robert Fitzgerald)

Oedipus is not only bitter toward his sons' indolence, but disgusted that they are not helping *him*. There is no willing self-abnegation in this hero, any more than in the raging Lear. Yet it is not simply interest which underlies Oedipus' hatred. It is the thought of the wrongs he has suffered in Thebes, immediately after the events related in *Oedipus Rex*; and it is the realization that Creon and Polyneices are only interested in regaining his support (or body) for what good it can do *them*. On two later occasions in the *Colonus* Oedipus expresses his loathing for his sons.

> These were the two
> Who saw me in disgrace and banishment
> And never lifted a hand for me. They heard me
> Howled from the country, heard the thing proclaimed.
> (427-30)

They cared more about their thrones than about their father's welfare. Later, when Polyneices has entered, the attack continues:

> Weeping is no good now. However long
> My life may last, I have to see it through;
> But I regard you as a murderer!
> For you reduced me to this misery,
> You made me an alien. Because of you
> I have begged my daily bread from other men. (1360-1364)

Oedipus attacks Creon still more violently (864-870): he curses even his brother-in-law's relatives, wishing them 'such days as I have had, and such an age as mine! ' It is of some interest that Antigone must remind her father to

Think of your mother's and your father's fate
And what you suffered through them! If you do,
I think you'll see how terrible an end
Terrible wrath may have. (1196-1198)

Yet from the outset of the play the features of a saint have been faintly visible. Others have shown a strange awe for Oedipus. His first self-revelation (219 ff.) is vastly impressive, frightening, and fascinating to the chorus of Athenians. Even earlier, when the chorus had first seen this unknown pilgrim, his appearance had shocked and upset them. When they have grown more used to him, they divulge their fascination:

Chorus:
What evil things have slept since long ago
It is not sweet to awaken;
And yet I long to be told –
Oedipus: What:
Chorus:
Of that heartbreak for which there was no help,
The pain you have had to suffer. (510-14)

It is still time before Oedipus starts behaving as though he were a saint, or as though he considered himself one. At that turning point we are led – by Sophocles' genius – through a convincing transition from the harshly secular to the more transcendent hero. One state flows easily into the other, until we feel that the final state was latent at the beginning. In each state Oedipus confronts his experience. This mood unifies. We turn, at the sound of thunder and lightning (1455 ff.), to a potentially transfigured man. He asks Antigone to bring Theseus, for

God's beating thunder, any moment now,
Will clap me underground: send for him quickly! (1460-1)

From this point on he seems to have left the human situation, which is still on all sides of him: he is in it, but no longer part of it. His words, like Christ's toward the end, have the strong echo of 'other places.' Oedipus still seems to proselytize indirectly for Athens, on behalf of Sophocles. This praise may jar, but in the context of the play it is perfectly fitting: the city of Athens has helped the saint, by taking its own spiritual stand. And the hero wants to leave a spiritual tradition behind him. Just as that wish seems to come from a man who is already beyond, so we feel, in Oedipus' brief final parting from Antigone and Ismene (1612-1617), that he addresses them with the calmness, even the recollective quality, of someone who has crossed a vast experience and can begin to think back from it

> Children, this day your father is gone from you
> All that was mine is gone. You shall no longer
> Bear the burden of taking care of me —
> I know it was hard, my children — And yet one word
> Makes all those difficulties disappear:
> That word is love . . .

The final moments of his mortal life, as the messenger recounts them, are strictly mysteries. The report of what could be seen elevates the sense of mystery. Oedipus had allowed only Theseus to see the final moments: Antigone, Ismene, and the messenger had withdrawn, and could see only Theseus,

> . . . only the king, his hands before his face,
> Shading his eyes as if from something awful,
> Fearful and unendurable to see. (1650-1652)

None of the other onlookers knew what had happened. It was no natural event — hurricane of lightning — the messenger assures us. It was either some 'attendant from the train of Heaven,' or

> . . . else the underworld
> Opened in love the unlit door of earth (1661-1662)

The mysterious end is a 'physical' confirmation of Oedipus' release from the human condition, a release which had already (l. 1455 ff) separated him from the beings around him. It takes him beyond the limits either of reason or of empirical wisdom.

ii

It may seem misleading to compare the literary treatment of Dionysus (in Euripides' *Bacchae*) with that of Oedipus. Dionysus was a part of divinity, Oedipus a man. It is quite obvious, though, that many 'divinities' on the Greek stage had about them little of the divine, in any sense of that troubled word. Think of Athena in the *Eumenides*; Heracles in the *Philoctetes*; Aphrodite or Artemis in Euripides' own *Hippolytus*; none of these deities has much inner majesty, power, or awesomeness. They seem no more divine than characters like Pelasgus or Neoptolemus. They are divine only in name. Dionysus in the *Bacchae* is an achievement of another order. It is not his reputation and status as a god, but the powerful characterization of him, from the inside out, that completes his divine aspect. His divinity is earned. As a verbal achievement, a translation of character from man into art, he is comparable to Oedipus.

The felt transcendence of Dionysus is much greater, throughout most of the play, than that of Oedipus in *Oedipus at Colonus*. We know at once that Dionysus is of a higher power than any of the other figures in his play. Unlike Oedipus, he never condescends to join the human scene. He is ruthless toward the unbelieving Pentheus. Even toward his followers he is, at kindest, ironic; by various indications from the chorus we know that they neither want nor expect from their divinity any of the tender emotions.

The dramatized transcendence of Dionysus is at its clearest in his treatment of Pentheus. We first notice the god playing with the ruler of Thebes: Dionysus refuses to take the human seriously. In this way he creates an awareness of his transcendence. It is the way of Christ at the marriage feast in Cana. Seeming to look down, though not to condescend; simply to understand the human from above, half in amusement, half in compassion. The mood is unsettling. The cult of Dionysus is, after all, close to play; and to earnest people nothing is more unsettling than play. Pentheus invites this treatment because of his moral earnestness, and his perfect acceptance of the propaganda of settled society. He is one of the eternal bourgeois of Balzac or Babbitt, one of those reified *salauds* whose pictures Roquentin studies in Sartre's *La Nausée*; pictures of men who have solidified their values beyond all loosening; for whom *nothing* of importance can ever again come into question. In their first dialogue Dionysus startles Pentheus by his irreverent, flippant dialectic (473-477):

Pentheus:
  Tell me the benefits
  That those who know your mysteries enjoy.
Dionysus:
  I am forbidden to say. But they are worth knowing.
Pentheus:
  Your answers are designed to make me curious.
Dionysus:
  No:
  Our mysteries abhor an unbelieving man.
Pentheus:
  You say you saw the god. What form did he assume?

Dionysus:

> Whatever form he wished. The choice was his, not mine.
> (Trans. of *Bacchae* by William Arrowsmith)

When this game proves too much for Pentheus he decides to use force, and imprisons Dionysus. This is the worst mistake. The outrage is promptly repaid. Pentheus believes that he has manacled and imprisoned Dionysus, who has then burned down the palace and escaped, while Dionysus claims that the entire imprisonment was a delusion of Pentheus, aided by Bacchus who burned the palace: in any case, it is a fact that the king's power has been made a joke. Nor for the last time. Dionysus, who emerges smiling and cool from the incinerated building, goes on to play his most extravagant trick. We know that he is finally acting only to prove his power and to win converts; but we admire the diabolical adroitness with which he goes on to destroy Pentheus. He plays sadistically on what, conveniently enough, turn out to be the young king's masochistic and voyeurish inclinations; a spell is cast on Pentheus, releasing him from self-control and inhibition. The god leads the 'sedate' king, now revealed to be a transvestite, up to the mountains, up to the Bacchantes' orgies. It is the absolute downfall of the bourgeois. Pentheus is beside himself with desire. But Dionysus has not finished. With cynical strategy he has warned his devotees of Pentheus' coming, and he leads them to the tree where the king is hiding. Then at the god's instigation the women destroy the king, tearing him apart. This *sparagmos* has the clearest possible religious overtones; the nonbeliever himself serving as the sacrificial host. Dionysus has manipulated the performance with grace and inner calm. He has not dirtied his hands.

Dionysus transcends very differently from Oedipus. Unlike Oedipus — and quite properly, considering his role as a 'god' — Dionysus remains consistently apart from the human. He does not work up through mortality, but consistently occupies a level above it. His mysteriousness, too, is something entirely his own. It is an uncanny mixture: beauty, power, and closeness to nature all converging strangely, even painfully, on ruthlessness, flippancy, and indifference to the human.

We have a working definition of literary transcendence; now we can ask, more critically, how rare transcendent characters are in Greek literature. At first it seemed easy to exclude drama-heroes like Orestes (in the *Oresteia*), or Prometheus. Does it still seem easy?

Among tragic Greek characters Prometheus comes closest, for

me, to rivalling the transcendent power of Oedipus and Dionysus. We would expect Aeschylus to provide such experience – more than Sophocles and Euripides – and it may be that in the complete *Prometheus* trilogy, of which we have only one third, he did just that. Even in *Prometheus Bound* the hero enters 'strange seas of thought,' challenging and steadily defying a Zeus whose designs are inscrutable, and working out to the extensive limits of his own inner geography. By identifying with Prometheus, and as far as possible following the course of his experience, we risk ourselves forward into issues which make our 'thought' anxious. We find ourselves wondering how divinity and suffering can be reconciled, and how intrinsically worthy the cause of mankind is. We find ourselves wondering what Prometheus makes us mean. There is a double process at work, in the experiencing of this play, which bears on our whole concern here. Prometheus – I hope the previous chapter made this clear – is far less human than Dionysus or Oedipus (in the *Colonus*). This may seem a paradox: earlier I stressed the transcendence of mortality, especially in Dionysus. But Oedipus and Dionysus are both immensely human in their more than human transcendence. This is evident in Oedipus, who is simultaneously a crotchety old man and a saint. Strangely enough the point holds even more firmly for Dionysus. His contempt for Pentheus, and his manipulation of his own personal effect, amount to patrician showmanship; with *this* phase of his behavior we identify, while we recognize an uncanniness, behind the showmanship, which removes the god from any conventional approach.

In contrast to both these figures Prometheus is pallid and abstract, though he embodies his abstraction powerfully. This abstractness, or forceful *conceptuality,* of Prometheus in his play-context, establishes the second part of the double process mentioned above. His character works itself off against schemata of such distinct, rational meaningfulness – in the quarrel between divinity and man – that the inexhaustible aspect of character is drained away into finite argument.

Orestes (in the *Oresteia*) owes even more to his context. Here we have a character of few established traits, projected by divinity into an urgent moral crisis: whether or not to murder his murderous mother. The moment in which we are most moved, by Orestes himself, is that in which he hesitates at Clytemnestra's threshold. Here he burrows into the mortal condition, digs to its roots; there is no 'going-beyond.' He most 'goes-beyond' in the *Eumenides,* when the gods choose him as proof that blood revenge must give way to adjudication by law. Yet by that time, Aeschylus has allowed him to lose what personality he had; the character has become simply a figure in a divine drama. He has lost the power to transcend, *as a character,* though he still illustrates Aeschylus' point about one way in which some of the weaknesses of the human can be transcended.

Transcendent characters are rare in Greek literature, as they are at all times, and in every literature. We can collect at most a handful from post-classical works: *Lear, Faust,* possibly in a strange way *Don Quixote.* The two previous chapters suggest there may have been very little of this sort of characterization in classical Greek literature. The production of such characters requires, of literary creators, a rare capacity to reflect onto the whole of human experience, as it presents itself both in themselves and in others. Then it involves a capacity to project into the moods and verbal strategems of 'going beyond.' The highest inward culture and the ripest technical maturity seem to be required here; as well, of course, as a rich ambient socio-economic culture. Our next question must be: what does such literary achievement, the flowering of tragedy, require of us?

> In tragedy myth severed its con-
> nexion with a particular concrete
> situation ... It is evident that this
> broadening of the perspective
> marks a tendency toward philoso-
> phical generalization.
>
> (Snell, *The Discovery of the Mind*)

Chapter IV

The Knowing of Greek Tragedy

Greek tragedy makes many demands on us; the first demand is upon what we might call our 'sympathy.' That sympathy, for the heroes of many Greek tragedies, is complex, as we have begun to see. As King Oedipus' tragedy unfolds we are made to experience con-flicting emotions toward him: we feel some of his own horror toward the self that he turns out to be, that same horror with which his friends, Jocasta and the chorus, finally regard him; but we also feel the rightness and nobility of his search for the self-knowledge which convicts him. We go in two directions. Our admiration for the hero's action, and our distress at his fate, are blended in a single feeling of sympathy. Even our horror toward Oedipus involves a feeling with him, especially because he feels a similar horror toward himself. According to various theories of the origin of tragedy, the rites which were later to develop into that genre presented a suffering hero who was both honored by the rite-creating community, and was their scapegoat, the bearer of their guilt. This communal sense of love and horror may be the historic model for the sympathy felt toward Oedipus. Don't our sympathies for Ajax, Philoctetes, or even Medea, to choose examples randomly from Greek tragedy, involve a certain revulsion together with a certain love? Couldn't this emotional joining be claimed for our experiencings of Pelasgus or Agamemnon (in *Iphigeneia*)?

Isn't there, furthermore, some *necessary* bond between the admiration and the horror which join in our sympathy for many tragic heroes? Aristotle believed that no satisfactory tragedy can involve the downfall of a wholly good man; also that we must not believe the tragic figure predestined to happiness. There is one obvious difficulty of Christian tragedy, that the Christian hero is *destined* to some kind of salvation after his suffering. (St. Evremond pointed this out conclusively). For the Greek tragic hero, on the other hand, the end is never certain; his greatest suffering is only a prelude to an awful and obscure after world – as was the case with the aged Oedipus. For this reason our sympathy with many ancient tragic heroes involves a love which is deepened by our ignorance and uncertainty of their destiny.

This thesis can be put much more strongly. Sympathy for a single hero is the chief response evoked by Greek tragedy; I have implied this already by stressing the central importance of dilemma, self-awareness, and transcendence. It is after all natural that a tragic hero, who originally emerged as a cynosure from the throng of the primitive chorus, should attract the chief interest of, and his suffering be the real concern of, the spectator of tragedy. Of course the hero's suffering is often part either of a chain of family sufferings, as in the *Oresteia,* or of a holocaust of sufferings, as in the *Persians* or *Seven Against Thebes.* And occasionally, in Euripidean plays like the *Trojan Women,* individual tragedy is totally merged into group tragedy. But all these plays in some degree obscure that genius of Greek tragedy which is to concentrate on a single hero, or at most on two, as in *Antigone.* By such concentration the Greek tragedian made the feeling of sympathy the chief end of his creation; a sympathy which grounded the deepest union of spectator with actor. Negatively, this point suggests one reason why Greek comedy does *not* awaken so much sympathy for its characters or situations: its themes are social processes or group situations – the founding of a utopian state, the spreading of new learning, women's attempt to win men to peace.

It follows that Greek comedy does not so clearly invite sympathy for its characters. (Or perhaps the emphasis, here, should be more emphatically on *characters*). Aristophanes tries more consciously than any major Greek writer, to enlist his audience's or reader's interest in a particular cause, as distinct from a character. In general, Aristophanes' causes are conservative: the old learning, an old-fashioned Zeus, the Athenian aristocracy, and pacifism – a topic especially objectionable to late fifth-century demagogues. And yet though he has a view for which he is pushing hard, his characters arouse relatively little sympathy, at least by contrast with the tragic effect. Aristophanes' characters awaken our sense of humor, our fascination with sex, our sense of the ridiculous; but in so doing they appeal chiefly to our faculties of 'criticism.' (I take that word to mean, in this case, 'judgment which is rational as far as aesthetic judgment can be'). The main characters displayed by Aristophanes are being centrally ridiculed in some manner: Socrates for his faith in progressive education; Pisthetairus for utopianism; Aeschylus for verbosity; Cleon for demagoguery. Aristophanes ridicules by criticizing characters as if they were living offenses to some norm: political, social, literary, or ethical. The audience's critical faculties are enlisted in a constant attempt to see 'difference' or 'otherness,' to compare and contrast. This is criticism functioning as critique. Aristophanic ridicule is sharply distinct from hatred. His ridicule arouses critical intellect, while hatred stifles it. Hatred, after all, is much closer to sympathy than it is to ridicule.

I feel sympathy toward the Greek tragic hero, whereas Aristophanes leads me into criticism; or rather Greek tragedy and comedy *tend* to reach for these ends. This brings us closer to the meanings of sympathy and criticism as they actually express themselves in Greek drama. Greek comedy presents normative situations in which certain actions or beliefs are criticized in terms of standards which make them appear wrong. Such criticism is effective because the characters whom Aristophanes ridicules have partially assimilated whole, coherent positions which stand or fall with them. When Socrates is discredited (in the *Clouds*) so is progressive education; when Aeschylus is spoofed for verbosity so are wordy people in general. There is a concrete universality in these comic characters. They are full and nonallegorical; but they are weighted with significance. Aristophanes constantly deals with ideas; and though they are fitted tightly to characters, like souls to bodies, his ideas can be plucked out and paraphrased with as little violence to literature as can ever be possible in this process. By doing this, his spectators could recreate the critical points that Aristophanes had created into his plays.

Violation of norms is not the source of the sympathy aroused by Greek tragedy; in fact the source of tragic sympathy is extremely hard to localize and describe. Generalizations about extant Greek tragedy are riskier than those about extant Greek comedy, because with the former we are left with three dramatists and nearly a century to consider, with the latter one dramatist and fifty years. On the whole, though, we can say that tragedy tends to awaken sympathy through the presentation of heroic characters—whose actions and sufferings demand evaluation, but *not* in terms of standards, ideas, or principles which those characters offend. Greek tragedy presents heroes whose experience calls for interpretation by laws, people who are breakers of new moral frontiers which will subsequently have laws but where none have yet been established. In this way tragedy awakens or uses our sympathies; they respond promptly to the inarticulate and precarious in the tragic hero's destiny. There is an integral bond between the sympathy of Greek tragedy and that drama's exploring quest for still unfound law or conceptual truth.

All this is especially clear in Sophocles' *Antigone* and *Oedipus the King*; plays which show two different degrees of the relation in tragedy between sympathy and non-rational quest. Aristophanes criticizes his characters in terms of his own ideas. Sophocles does not criticize, in that sense; rather he casts, into an eventually criticizable light, the actions of Antigone and Oedipus, of Philoctetes, Ajax, or Deianira. But how does Sophocles go about this? We can guess the answer from the mass of contradictory interpretations which critics have foisted onto *Antigone* and *Oedipus the King*. Sophocles has somehow left the concepts that he handled, and which his characters enact or seek to discover, roughedged and incomplete; and he seems to have done this by a kind of unconscious purpose.

In *Antigone* he considers the conflict between duties toward the state and duties toward religion. Most people today feel that Antigone herself is the most important and sympathetic character in the play; and yet that feeling is part of our historical conditioning. Sophocles never negates the impression, created by the entire play, that both Creon and Antigone speak for universally valid attitudes in the quarrel of state with religion. This is true even when Creon is most short-sighted and cruel to Antigone and Haemon: at those points Creon seems to be failing his own ideal of the statesman, which he describes to Antigone early in the play; and yet it is plainly Creon and not the ideal which is failing. It is the same with the character of Antigone; her ideal is not dirtied by what is petulant and silly in her actions, but rather remains poised in perfectly pure hostility to the ideal of state philosophy. This perfect poise led Hegel, in *The Phenomenology of Mind*, to say that in *Antigone* Sophocles presents an irreconcilable conflict between two ideals. But just because the conflict is of that sort, the individual tragedies involved in Sophocles' play have a significance which is on a level different from that of the ideal quarrel raging above them. The meaning of the particular meeting of Antigone with Creon, on the issue of body-burying, is not clarified by our knowing the ideals which are simultaneously but immovably involved; although that meeting is heightened and charged by such knowledge. In this sense there is in *Antigone* a disassociation of ideal from character.

The ideals in *Antigone* are bodies of principles – concerning state or God – just as the ideas which compound Aristophanes' characters were bodies of principles – concerning peace or education. The striking point, here, is the contrast between the relative disassociation of ideal from character in *Antigone* and the relative unity of idea and character in Aristophanes. Not only is each character in Aristophanes – Socrates, Lysistrata, Dicaeopolis – a bearer of conceptual attitudes, but he is so in such a way that attitude or idea will fall simultaneously with his character. However in *Antigone* the norms or ideals, which are available for the conceptual judging of character, tend finally to be irrelevant to that judgment. Thus there results in our reflection on that play a kind of ideal-character dualism, which is hard to realize in the concrete experiencing of the play. But to the extent it is realized there our sympathy for Antigone herself is diffused by the realization of her conceptual 'significance.' And to the extent that Antigone's vital being, and not her point of view, is foremost, she becomes one of the most sympathetic figures in Greek literature. Though even then, we feel, there is something unexplorative and prefigured about her personal destiny; it has at least the inexorability of ideas.

I began with *Antigone,* in contrasting certain aims of Aristophanes' and Sophocles' drama. *Antigone* is the one play of Sophocles' in which the characters might seem to be vehicles of ideas in the sense in which they are that in Aristophanes. But in fact the difference from Aristophanes is evident. Sophocles is far less conceptual than Aristophanes. Yet Sophocles himself is far more conceptual in *Antigone* than in *Oedipus the King,* my last example here. Already in *Antigone* we can see what is the finest characteristic of Sophoclean tragedy: its search for ideas and truth through drama, as end results of it. Character and concept are tightly joined, but the latter is deeply enriched by the former. By embodying this search in drama Sophocles calls on our exploring aesthetic faculty, that sympathy with which we had seen ourselves drawn into the experience of the old Oedipus' transcendence, in *Oedipus at Colonus.* Aristophanes embodied ideas and truth themselves, as he saw them, in his plays. For him a play was an occasion for seeing confirmations of what we should already know, not an occasion for learning.

In *Oedipus the King* Sophocles considered only one tragic hero, Oedipus. Oedipus and his tragedy are made so deeply sympathetic that nothing else in the play really matters. (We discussed this in the preceding chapter). Our sympathy for Oedipus is complex enough to include the notion that he has committed great crimes. Oedipus and I both think that there is something revolting about him. This is appropriate. The wretchedness which Sophocles inflicts on his hero, at the end of his play, would be intolerable if we did not feel it was somehow deserved. So a crucial and appropriate question to ask about the play is this: exactly what does Sophocles think that Oedipus has done to deserve his downfall? He offers one obvious incriminating fact, that Oedipus has killed his father and married his mother. But why has Oedipus done this? His personality lent itself to these particular acts. However it lent itself primarily because the gods, through oracles, had predestined the chain of events described in the play. Character and oracle meet in Oedipus. Sophocles implies that the gods shaped fate that way because Oedipus had a particular character, but not that the gods through predestination changed the character of Oedipus, leading him to fulfill their fate. In this qualified sense Oedipus seems responsible for his tragedy. It is impoverishing to think of this play as a treatise on predestination, but it is still obvious that fate or destiny is central in the bringing on of Oedipus' tragic downfall. What he has done is simply to be Oedipus at a destined moment.

His responsibility and his non-responsibility are interwoven. The non-responsibility is carefully suggested. We ask: couldn't Jocasta and Laius have made surer that their son was really killed when they exposed him after birth? Or couldn't Oedipus have avoided the oracle, when he was young, by finding out who his mother and father really were? Possibly the oracle could have been outtricked by more perseverance, but the ironic fact is that all attempts to escape the oracle led right into the fulfilling of it: Jocasta and Laius did put their son out alive into the wide world, and Oedipus did leave home. In other words, the gods actively wanted to prevent an evasion of the oracles. But this does not mean that fate is simply avenging itself on the basically worthy Oedipus. On the contrary, the fact that he is sympathetic shows that he has a character of his own; it is incompatible with the notion that the gods are merely taking revenge on him. In fact Oedipus is a hero of the will, it being true of him that he brought on, by his own nature, his own suffering. One way to describe the balance of hero with destiny in this play would be this: to say that Oedipus is honored, not violated, by being trapped, by being allowed to entrap himself in a significant web of sin. As a great searcher for self-knowledge it is his privilege to come to the highest, even if most painful, realization of the meaning of his life. *Oedipus at Colonus* amplifies this point, as we have seen. But *Oedipus the King* proves enough. There Sophocles heroizes Oedipus by showing his willing invocation of god-fated destiny. The result has transcendent implications. For the appearance of inevitability in *Oedipus the King* gives the events of the play the kind of grandeur which events in history can seem to us to have: they are perfected, in a sense, because though they do not show the limitations of necessity, it is impossible to think that they could have taken place otherwise.

Thus in the person of Oedipus Sophocles offers a living and vital character whose tragedy raises and phrases transcendent questions, rather than answering questions or being the affirmation of a reasonable position. This is meant to face two ways: back toward my earlier remarks on *Oedipus the King,* and forward toward a statement of why Oedipus is unjudgable and uninterpretable by concepts. When I said that Aristophanes makes his spectator constantly aware of otherness and difference, I meant that he did this by presenting characters with a meaning or significance which could be contrasted with other meanings. We can find concepts to describe the points of view which Aristophanes' characters are, and which Aristophanes variously criticizes. But the character of Oedipus accumulates whatever meaning he has through his action toward or into the realm of the divine. His actions are measurable not by other men's actions but by the way in which they define themselves into the higher realities of the world, the Greek divine. If Oedipus is to be judged, to be measured by norms, it must be by divine norms. Now the characteristic mark of the Greek divine is that it had being only as explored by the personal, that is by the pantheon of mythological gods or legendary heroes. Thus through Greek tragedy, for example, the divine could be continually recreated and reinterpreted. In a sense the divine only meant what it *was* when reflected in fictive beings.

This possibility was most fully developed in Homer, while by the fifth century, it is true, philosophies like those of *nous* and *moira,* as Anaxagoras held them, could be cast in more statically metaphysical language. However Greek tragedy remained, in its function as central religious experience for the whole Greek people, a search for, rather than an affirmation of, divine laws. Mythology, both that of the pantheon and of the legendary houses and figures with whom tragedy dealt, remained a concrete and mobile means of organization of religious experience for the Greek art of the fifth century.

We come to understand that although fate is involved in Oedipus' tragedy, it is a fate which is personal, like the gods with whom the Greeks peopled the divine. This fate has meaning for our play only as it is a fate created, and given substance to, through the chief person in the play. Apart from Oedipus himself the fate which caught him has no existence. The drama of Oedipus is a kind of discourse about fate, inspired by Sophocles' desire to understand fate better, and to articulate ideas about it. Or, changing descriptions, we could say that *Oedipus the King* is an inquiry into a problem within the terms which the play itself establishes for that problem. This is the sense in which I mean that the character of Oedipus raises questions. He himself cannot be judged in terms of norm-ideas until the play ends, because his tragic actions must themselves be the ideas in question.

To the extent that we fall with Oedipus, in his discovery of his sin and in his subsequent suffering, we prepare ourselves for asking a cluster of questions of which the whole play is the preliminary statement. What is the relation of sin to nobility? What is the relation of free-will to fate? What kind of dignity resides in self-knowledge? The way in which we come to ask these questions, through the very experience of the play, suggests again how the relation of character to idea in *Oedipus the King* differs from that relation in *Antigone* and in Aristophanes' comedy. In the *Clouds* Socrates was a body of principles which he represented. In *Antigone* there was a split between character, and ideas or principles; the fates of those two dramatic factors weren't completely interdependent. In *Oedipus the King,* however, we almost entirely miss intelligible principles or norms informing the play and enriching character. We are introduced to a crucial situation in a noble individual's life, and are forced to experience, to feel, his tragedy with him. One final way of describing the difference of *Oedipus the King* from the *Clouds,*

then, would be to say that the former would be much more
denatured than the latter in a conceptual, prose summary. In this
comparison *Antigone* would be a mean between the extremes. The
other plays we have considered, in earlier chapters, would on this
spectrum lie somewhere between *Antigone* and *Oedipus*.

The last question is this: what is the philosophical importance
of the union, in our experience of Greek tragedy, between sympathy
and the questing exploration of new realms of spiritual experience?
This sympathy is not transmitted by ideas but by a kind of inter-
penetrative process through which spectator and tragic hero are
united. It marks this transaction that through it we can search for
knowledge by a continual, never fully articulated, series of questings.
In the search we may be asking ourselves: what is the meaning of
decision; of free will; of incest; of love? But in each case, during the
tragic transaction, we are simply forming these questions, and hoping
for the leaven of eventual concepts; we are not dealing with achieved
ideas. Thus it is important, in the bond which establishes our sympathy for the tragic quest, that it exhibits a kind of nascent, struggling, and profound inquiry, an inquiry which we both can and
cannot call cognitive. This inquiry is too preparatory to be cognitive
in the ordinary sense. It is too nearly just a forming of concepts. But
the tragic quest is cognitive at least in the sense of being an experiencing into, and a learning about, its own content. It is an articula-
tion of searching questions about the world in which we find ourselves.

> The poet who has the divine gift of anabiosis must, like Homer, be a master of the art of creating a second illusion, the Illusion of Vitality.
>
> (Bassett, *The Poetry of Homer*)

Chapter V

Objectivity in Homer

Out from the matrix of its characterizations, and especially of its characterizations viewed in action, Greek tragedy arranges to lead us toward transcendence and wisdom, or at least into the questions which might lead to those realizations. Its method is to engage us, precariously and through our sympathies, with situations which take us profoundly beyond what we usually are, or beyond the ways we usually define ourselves. Tragedy does this by building on a long preparatory stage of literary character-deepening and awareness, of which we have seen some selected moments in fifth-century Greek literature. In particular we have seen dilemma and self-awareness developed to bring out certain profundities of character. We let Pelasgus, Neoptolemus, Prometheus, Oedipus and Dionysus tell us about these matters.

In such ways Greek tragedy adventures its readers into unexpected and unplotted domains of experience. It does this more obviously than Greek comedy, though in a broader sense these dramatic genres, or sub-genres, are one in nature. That unity seems even clearer when Greek epic is brought under study, for epic work is sharply different from dramatic. Epic began, and on the whole remained, objectifying, holding its experiencer at a distance, not 'drawing him in.' In one sense – of direct historical continuity – epic inherited the Near Eastern world, through Phoenicia and Mycenae, more directly and fully than Greek tragedy did. But that phase of inwardliness gave itself even more fully to lyric and drama than to epic. It passed into the early stages of Greek tragedy. The reasons, we shall see, may be rather closely tied to the formal demands of the individual genres.

Homer's language is formal and 'objectifying.' His dactylic

hexameter is farther from the cadence of normal speech than are either trochee or iamb, the main building-blocks of lyric and tragedy. The opening lines of the *Iliad*

Μῆνιν ἄειδε Θεά Πηληιάδεω 'Αχιλῆος
οὐλομένην ἣ μυρί Ἀχαιοῖς ἄλγε' ἔθηκε

or even of the *Aeneid,*

Arma virumque cano, Troiae qui primus ab oris
Italiam fato profugus Lavinaque venit . . .,

signalled the introduction to an 'artificial,' nonconversational experience. No doubt this was true even by contrast to Dante's

Nel mezzo del cammin di nostra vita
mi ritrovai per una selva oscura
che la diritta via era smarrita,

or to Milton's

Of man's first disobedience and the fruit
Of that forbidden tree, whose mortal taste. . .

'Grand' and 'exigent' Milton's cadence seems to us; still it has a quality of heightened and dignified speech. Ancient epic language, for reasons partly of its religious background, was consciously removed from speech, relatively near the language of rite. We hear that older sound in every line of Homer.

Verbal formulae widen the distance of Homeric language from daily speech. These tailor-made organizations of sound and meaning – all the 'winged words,' 'rosy-fingered dawns,' and 'well-greaved Achaeans' – facilitated composition in a metrically rigorous form like the dactylic hexameter. Formulaic phrases used repeatedly in more or less the same form fitted themselves into the metrical pattern of the line. It has been estimated by Denys Page 'that about one-fifth of the Homeric poems is composed of lines wholly repeated from one place to another, and that in some 28,000 lines there are some 25,000 repeated phrases.'[1]

Formulaic language is far removed from ordinary speech, with its more irregular patterns; formulae give language a hieratic quality which is lacking in most conversation, or in literature closely derived from conversation. To this factor must be added the weight of mere verbal repetition. The Homeric vocabulary is relatively small. In fact

1. Denys Page, *History and the Homeric Iliad* (Berkeley, 1959), p. 223.

the word, as such, is not interesting, is not a basic element of Homeric language: only the *kolon*, the metrical unit or group of words, the phrase, is basic. Homer manipulates these units, combined and recombined with infinite ingenuity. His ingenuity makes his repetition effective, makes it *the* distinctive effect of his poetry, but it does not lessen the impression of the repeated, the ritually emphasized, in his epic. Such ritual quality has never since been so effectively used to separate poetic language from the casualness of speech.

Homer's language is objective and formal; in addition, his vocabulary is artificial, is far removed from everyday vocabulary. This point, too, has bearing here; it interweaves with and colors the entire character of the *Iliad* and *Odyssey*. Whatever the explanation, the vocabulary of the *Iliad* appears on the whole to be synthetic, a combination of Ionic and Aeolic dialects. There are various reasons for thinking that Homer did not write in a homogeneous dialect. For instance, he seems frequently to have more than one word for the same thing: he often uses synonyms, In many cases, furthermore, he has preferred exclusively the forms of one or the other dialect for a specific word, even when a word in the other dialect was available; elsewhere he has indiscriminately used the forms of either dialect for the same word. So it has been necessary to abandon one appealing theory: that Homer's own dialect was essentially Aeolic, and that later editors tried to 'translate' the Homeric poems into Ionic. There is a too systematic and deeply interwoven mixture of dialects in Homeric epic as we have it. Not only that, but there are unmistakable traces of very old Arcadian and Cypriote dialects, as well as some puzzling, seemingly Attic forms embedded in the verse. For all these reasons we have to suppose that Homer was composing (and writing) in a composite, artificial dialect, presumably created by a long bardic tradition. If, as seems likely, he was a native of Chios, living in the eighth-century, he would have been a natural heir to such an aritifical *Kunst-Sprache*: he would have been living close to Aeolic (on Lesbos), to Ionic (the chief dialect of the Asia Minor seabord), and of course also to Cypriote. It remains imaginable that he might have inherited a linguistic tradition so ancient that it predated the separation of Aeolic from Ionic (before 1000 B.C.). But that is unlikely.

2. For more detail cf. A. Meillet, *Aperçu d'une histoire de la langue grecque* (Paris, 1930).

These linguistic points take their place in a larger truth: that Homer's fundamental verbal self-expression is formal, artificial (in a sense), and objective or impersonal; that it is directed away from personal, conversational communication. In several of these points, though not the last, he sets his work at considerable distance from classical tragedy.

These points themselves can become elements in a larger argument. We are limited in our knowledge of the bardic tradition in early Greece. Yet there is no doubt that Homer, and the other early epic writers, composed works to be recited or sung. (Bowra and others have argued for a kind of singing.) This of course does not distinguish Homer from such later poets as Archilochus, Pindar, or Bacchylides. They all composed works which would be publicly recited to musical accompaniment. By the fifth century, however, it seems that the bardic tradition properly devoted to the singing of epic is dying out, and is being replaced by a rhapsode tradition, led by singers of shorter pieces, especially of lyrics. Such rhapsodes are products of the age of greater individualism. The epic bardic tradition was far more impersonal, more involved with suprapersonal values and points of view. Its material was that vast, continuous body of epic lays which we call the epic cycle. Its antiquity was vast, and its authors largely unknown. Its matter was public property and encouraged subordination of the artist to his art. Whether we prefer to imagine Homeric verse recited in the halls of wealthy feudal aristocrats, or at vast, public Panionic festivals, as Wade-Gery believes,[3] we shall have to agree that such verse was produced under public conditions which seriously affected it, which helped to give it, as a genre, a character very much its own. We have not yet been stressing the social dimension of Greek literature. But we will come back to that crucial issue later.

Through his epic language Homer creates a 'world.' In that world, as Schiller said, the author seems to be present only as God is present in His creation. The author is evenly distributed. The objectivity of Homer's creation could hardly be realized more fully. What is worldlike about Homer's creation in the *Iliad*? [4]

3. H. T. Wade-Gery, *The Poet of the Iliad* (Cambridge, 1952).
4. Two nonacademic works dramatize the "sense of an independent world" in Homer: Rachel Bespaloff, *On the Iliad*, trans. Mary McCarthy (New York, 1947), and Simone Weill, *The Iliad or the Poem of Force* (Politics Pamphlet No. 1, New York).

A vision established in dactylic hexameters is not subjective, at least fights against subjectivity. There is bound to be, and in Homer there is, much objective space and much objective time: all of it distinctly 'out there.' It is true that the scene of the *Iliad* is set in few places: on the battlefield; before the Greek ships; on the Trojan ramparts. But it is remarkable, especially on the battlefield, that a sense of great space – and a great sense of space – is aroused. The geography of the battlefield is imprecise: we experience the combat of the *Iliad* with no other inner landmarks than the Trojan Walls, the tree before them, the Greek ships, the wall and the ditch before them. Between the opposing forces there is undifferentiated space awaiting action to define it. The vastness of that area is dramatized by a number of individual fights. It is insisted that many things are going on simultaneously. Who has equalled Homer in such insistence? Perhaps only Stendhal, in the description of Waterloo in *La Chartreuse de Parme;* or Tolstoy on the battle of Moscow in *War and Peace.*

The *Iliad* also establishes a definite sense of the passing of objective time. (Whereas in tragedy the past seems always to be an urging present). Looking to a modern parallel for contrast, we come on Proust. Where he treats time as a subjective experience, a function of memory, Homer projects time strictly away from the creative self, giving time a startling autonomy. He does *not* accomplish this by a realistic calendar chronology. His chronology is so obscure that we can hardly determine the time taken by the events of the *Iliad.* Large parts of the roughtly seven-week span of the epic are passed over rapidly: other parts are examined in detail. But the feeling of objective temporal reality is strongly manipulated. The weariness of successively wounded heroes, even the monotony of language with which their woundings are described, contributes to the temporal effect. Such reminiscences as those of Nestor, in Book XI, make the past seem real, an independent fact. Or on a larger scale: the seemingly interminable fighting, which transpires during the few hours between Book XI (Agamemnon's feats) and Book XVI (the sally of Patroklos), makes time into a pervasive external trait of the poem. The burdensomeness of time, there established, is not transmitted through the feelings of any of the characters fighting; it is made to seem, in the *Iliad,* as independently real as anything in the epic.

In this large spatio-temporal world Homer, like God leaning

over His world, has placed a great number of people. The *Iliad* teems
with soon-to-be forgotten names. These characters are not indivi-
dually decisive. Yet the countless names who fight and die forgotten,
say in Books XIV and XV, contribute to the sense of a real world,
seem projected from their author far out into objectivity. Here again
Homer resembles Tolstoy, or the Pasternak of *Doctor Zhivago*. He
infuses a sense of autonomous existence into his world, through the
crowd of lesser characters with whom he fills it.

However it is important to see that these characters are integrated into the poetic texture of Homer's world, and that they are
fully 'alive.' (Where 'aliveness' has something to do with subjectivity,
with 'having a self.') Their degree and kind of vitality is illustrated by
certain minor figures of *Iliad* XI. The servant-girl Hekamede, who
tends Nestor and Machaon, has a strange (not general) freshness and
sweetness. This is enhanced by her context: in a haven, only shortly
separated in mood and space from the sweat of the war. That is, this
character's life is to be understood in its context in the epic world.
The effect is the same with Eurypylos, whom Patroklos meets after
he leaves Nestor. Eurypylos, a seldom emphasized (though potent)
hero, is vitally touching (ll. 809 -812),

> limping
> away from the battle, and the watery sweat was running
> down his shoulders and face, and from the sore wound dark blood
> continued to drip, and yet the will stayed steady within him.

(Translations of Homer by Richmond Lattimore)

In itself this description is not unusually touching. But it follows the
series-wounding of the Greek heroes, and the urgent pleas of Nestor:
for the moment, desperation gives the description of Eurypylos a
unique vitality. Finally, one of the Trojans killed by Agamemnon in
Book XI: Iphidamas, son of Antenor. Like many of the lesser heroes
who are killed, Iphidamas is given a brief but distinctive biography.
In this instance the touching note is that

> Iphidamas fell there and went into the brazen slumber,
> unhappy, who came to help his own people, and left his young wife
> a bride, and had known no delight from her yet, and had given much
> for her.

There is a distinctive pathos here. Yet the fate of Iphidamas is so
relevant, so related, to that of many who die on both sides, that it
has adequate meaning *only* in its context. The pathos does not
intrude.

This point, that Homer gives life to his minor characters, but only by projecting them into the objective world of his creation, illustrates itself among more prominent characters. Nestor is an example. At first he talks so freely, launches so willingly into leisured observations, even under desperate circumstances, that we take the old man to be a stock character, a typical blowhard. In Book XI, for example, he detains Patroklos with an interminable story about his own boyhood courage. We only gradually realize that the story has detailed relevance to the present situation of the epic, that it is integrated. Nestor is calling on Achilles to behave with the same courage and sense of honor which he himself showed as a youth. Nestor does not, for all his relevance as a structural factor here, lose either vitality or individuality. But he is severely integrated into the text's whole, losing any trace of character which might project beyond the surface of the work which contains him. He never emerges onto us, like Oedipus or Medea in the plays containing (or trying to contain) them.

Nestor's double nature, as simultaneously a character and a strictly functional element of the poem, is brought out in another story which he narrates. In Book VII (124-169) he urges the Greeks, mainly Achilles, to meet Hector's challenge to a single combat. As in Book XI, Nestor implies a contrast between his own bravery, in youth, and that of the mature Greek warriors who are shirking the war. The speech has three parts. It opens with an appeal to the judgment of Peleus – indirectly aimed at Achilles (124-131) – and passes on, through the link of the personal association of Nestor and Peleus, to the familiar introductory, 'I wish that I were mighty, as when on the swift Keladon' (133). Having returned in time to his own childhood Nestor describes, from a carefully selected point of view, a conflict between the Pylians and Arcadians. The description of the battle occupies some six lines (151-156), but the bulk of the passage (136-150) is an account of the history of Ereuthalion's armor. This simple history within a history adds significance to the armor which Nestor's opponent wears in the battle, especially since Areithoos and Lykoorgos were properly warlike. The power of the armor and the power of its wearers are interfused.

The battle itself is simply young Nestor's defeat of Ereuthalion. The second part of the speech concludes with the 'would that I were mighty' (157), and Nestor follows it with a brief contrast between himself, who would have enjoyed answering Hector's challenge, and the best of the Greeks, who are afraid to answer it. Like the speech in Book XI, this Nestorian speech is a fusion of engaging story and reference to the past, with direct contribution to the structural progress of the poem; calling on Achilles as it does, and reminding the Greeks of the strong warriors in history. The speech in Book XI, however, is fitted to a leisurely personal interchange, while this one in Book VII has the brevity needed for an address to the assembled chiefs. No distinction is possible, in either of the speeches of Nestor in Books XI and VII, between relevant plot and ornamental digression; the two are intimately woven together.

I am arguing for the considerable, and muting, integration of character into the whole verbal texture, and the whole world, of the Homeric epic. In doing this I mean to stress the difference between Greek epic and the far more existentially demanding genre of Greek tragedy. Yet even on this general level the case has not been closed. If any character in the *Iliad* tests, and in fact threatens, the present argument, it is Achilles. For he has an existential immediacy which we normally associate only with the greater figures of Greek tragedy, or with the *personae* of the greatest Greek lyric poets. We have to consider this threat.

To a considerable extent, thanks to Homer's strict control, Achilles is restricted to his function. This hero's anger, as Homer promises in the first line of the epic, is the theme of the *Iliad;* and around that anger, as around a soul, revolves the unity of much of the work of the *menis*, or wrath theme, the oldest stratum of the *Iliad*. Most of the *menis* portion – all that precedes the announcement to Achilles of the death of Patroklos – is motivated by Achilles' anger. His request to Thetis, that the Greek forces should be driven back, determines the overall movement of Trojan success, a movement which Achilles self-satisfiedly observes in Book XI. Admittedly, the *menis* theme is only scattered through the first half of the epic: in Books I, IX, XI. But in that oldest stratum of the poem Achilles dominates. Furthermore, Homer has fused the spirit of the curse of Achilles with the entire mood of the fighting in the first half of the epic. Achilles' presence is everywhere. His wrath reaches even farther, too, actually determining the events which follow Patroklos' death. There the wrath has been redirected. It is no longer aimed against the Greeks, or even against Agamemnon. The loss of Patroklos has driven out that hatred. Suddenly Achilles realizes how deeply he is implicated in the war. By agreeing to let Patroklos fight, he has taken his stance. From now on he will turn his fury against the Trojans. The final six books are the consequence of that anger, which functions as the dynamic principle of the entire epic.

To this extent the character of Achilles fits into the objective, context-bound treatment of character in Homeric epic. Of course even as a functional element Achilles is potent, of crucial structural importance. Yet he is successfully distanced: between him and us there is immense psychic distance.

However Achilles is not entirely a 'functional character.' More than any other character in the *Iliad* or *Odyssey* he has an arbitrary quality which makes him stand out from his text. His original wrath, his consequent sulking, his sorrow for Patroklos, are all motivating events. Structurally, they are necessary. They are, however, much more than necessary. Homer has created a pathological, over-responsive character. From the outset, Achilles' wrath is excessive. He is unnecessarily ready to attack Agamemnon. He is too quick to remember his former wrongs at Agamemnon's hands: a brooding history. Achilles' brooding is excessive, although in a sense he is in the right, until the Embassy comes to him in Book XI. That expression of Agamemnon's desire to relent burdens Achilles with the responsibility of changing his mood. He confesses his inability to do so by taking surprising refuge in a general principle. Instead of angrily rebuffing the ambassadors he speaks of the futility of all war, the impossibility of knowing that one will get his fair share, and so forth. He is trying to make the anger, which is transparently at the source of his mood, inaccessible to argument. He has not turned philosopher. We find him wavering between alternatives: of sailing away the next morning; or of helping the Greeks — if their desperation becomes great enough. His sorrow for Patroklos shows him most exceeding the response necessary to the continued motivation of the epic. Achilles' weeping and rolling on the ground, at the death of his friend, drive him forcefully out through the restraining verbal texture of the work. They drive him, with a force rare in any epic, toward the existential immediacy of the tragic-dramatic character, or of the intense lyric *persona*. This is even truer of Achilles' treatment of Hector. The revenge taken on Patroklos' killer is no central motivational element. The poem is nearly over. We see there, in special purity, the arbitrariness and excessiveness of Achilles' character, which reaches out beyond the structural demands of the *Iliad*.

Here, too, is the crowning feature of Achilles' vitality: his self-consciousness. From Homer on, that self-awareness plays an increasingly important role in the development of Greek literature. I have considered the matter already, as it presents itself in *Prometheus Bound,* and will return directly to it in a later chapter on Solon Homer projects relatively little self-awareness into his work; his characters have little reflexive dimension. Of course this point needs qualifying.[5] We all know the frightful scene (Book XXII, 99 ff.) in which Hector is debating before the Trojan walls whether to flee or to face Achilles. He considers his responsibilities at length and in detail. This is a kind of 'self-awareness.' On a less elaborate scale there are many comparable self-investigations. Achilles wonders whether or not to strike Agamemnon; Helen, on the Scaean Gates, wonders why she left home; Achilles, at the end, wonders what he can do against the attacking river-god. I am struck by the formality and externality of these inner dialogues with the self. They are small, formal debates. They do not tear us with them, like the dilemmas of Agamemnon, Pelasgus, or Neoptolemus. Unique for Homeric epic, though, is the self awareness of Achilles.

Already in the first book he shows us an inner dimensionality lacking to the other characters. In the startling intensity of that book there is no time for examining; Achilles becomes clearer only in the leisurely embassy of Book IX. In the context of that book all attention is on him. Odysseus, Phoenix, and Ajax have come only to make an impression on Achilles' apparently impregnable mind. All thoughts center on that mind. Yet Achilles himself turns within a completely self-enclosed world. He *is* impregnable to argument. This need not necessarily mean that he is self-aware. But the mode of self-relatedness, in which Achilles here exists, is the condition for self-awareness. It is the condition out of which, for instance, he will later be able to report on his own condition with an inwardliness which is found nowhere else in the *Iliad.* In Book XVIII, just after having learned of the death of Patroklos, and in conversation with the sympathizing Thetis, Achilles repeats the prophecy that he is destined to early death if he continues to fight. 'As it is,' he says to Thetis (88 -92),

> there must be on your heart a numberless sorrow
> for your son's death, since you can never again receive him

---

5. There has been some qualification: cf. J. Böhme, *Die Seele und das Ich im homerischen Epos* (Leipzig-Berlin, 1929).

won home again to his country; since the spirit within does not drive me
to go on living and be among men except on condition
that Hektor first be beaten down under my spear.

Or, shortly after (98 -99):

I must die soon, then; since I was not to stand by my companion when he
was killed.

No more comment is needed, here, on the thoroughness of
Achilles' self-knowledge. Its poignancy — for this is no mere formula
he is repeating — impresses itself on us a few lines later. Generalizing
his own discouragement, Achilles says wearily (107 -110):

Why, I wish that strife would vanish away from among gods and mortals,
and gall, which makes a man grow angry for all his great mind,
that gall of anger that swarms like smoke inside of a man's heart
and becomes a thing sweeter to him by far than the dripping of honey.

Homer's Agamemnon will come to realize that a certain blind-
ness (*ate*) originally made him offend Achilles. But being a character
of little inner life, and great public responsibility, he will never
express an adequate sensuous or metaphorical, or even intellectual,
grasp of his inner problem. Homer does not take that kind of interest
in Agamemnon. (Euripides took much more). Achilles rises, in the
passage above, to what is for Greek epic an unprecedentedly honest
self-analysis. The bittersweetness of his brooding is apparent to him.
There is more such in the last book. There, in the encounter with
Priam, the hero again turns in on himself. (That his mind's motion is
here inward, more than outward, frustrates critics who want the final
Achilles to be more a generously 'Christian' hero than he is.) In fact
he thinks of his father, a thought which, as Priam suspects, will be
mellowing. More deeply, though, Achilles thinks of himself as a
person-who-has-a-father, as one who is part of the mortal condition.
And just as the hero's thought of his fated death mellows him, and
he longs for an end to the fighting, so here he is calmed by his
awareness of the human situation in which he, though part immortal,
participates.

It is difficult to study characterization in the *Iliad*, and the
extent to which Homer's characters, like the later figures of Greek
tragedy, acquire genuine existential immediacy. Samuel Bassett has
made a case for the deeply dramatic quality of Homer's own epic
verse. In *The Poetry of Homer* he remarks that:

if the verses which introduce the speeches and are little more than the stage direction 'loquitur' of drama are included, three-fifths of Homer consists of speeches. This is almost exactly the same proportion as that of speech to choral lyrics in the *Suppliants* of Aeschylus.[6]

This situation is of more than formal importance. Continually, as in the Embassy (Book IX) or in Achilles' hut when Priam has come, Homer establishes a 'dramatic' context, an appropriate environment which seems perfectly stageable. Bassett himself draws up an ingenious outline for staging the Niptra (*Iliad* XIX). At the same time he sees the likelihood that Homer, of whose work some of Aeschylus' tragedies were apparently 'slices,' had great influence on tragedy.

Despite this argument and imaginable extensions of it, stressing the intensely dramatic power of Achilles, the analogy between drama and epic cannot be pushed as far as Bassett pushes it. The entire context of any part of the *Iliad*, beginning with the basic verbal stratum, has to be considered. There is no reason to isolate certain elements of the poem, except in order to distinguish its now fused but originally separate divisions. This belief, of course, rests on a unitarian view of the epic. But that is also Bassett's view, so it is reasonable to criticize his isolation of episodes in the *Iliad.* Those episodes have no existence. They are patterns in a single, homogeneous verbal making. They are composed of the same metrical *kola* as the rest of the *Iliad.* They are experienced — and we have to imagine the original experience of *listening* to Homer — not as isolated units, but as parts of a whole. The difficulty with the drama theory does not end here. For even on a supraverbal level, one experienced concurrently with the verbal, the Homeric character is part of a large world. That world keeps him at an appropriately diminutive level. We feel we are looking down from a mountain. The epic world surrounds man, in a full spatio-temporal universe, with multitudes of things, people, and attitudes which are not himself. It puts upon almost every salience or uniqueness, a sharp tax of relevance. I have indicated how, in Book XI, Homer demands this tax of every character; conspicuously of Nestor, who might at first seem to stand out from the poem, and many of whose speeches have been considered interpolations. Relevance of course, is equally necessary in drama. But there much enters, outside the tight verbal texture

6. Samuel E. Bassett, *The Poetry of Homer* (Cambridge, 1939), pp. 59-60.

which constitutes Homeric epic. Scene, costume, gesture play their parts. The notion of internal relevance grows broad and loose. There is more room for chance and arbitrary organization than in epic. There is far more existential immediacy, which finally, in part, bursts structure.

Even to Homer's Achilles I denied what I called the existential immediacy of the dramatic characters. This denial was not evaluative. It involved no judgment on Achilles, Homer, or the epic. In fact we began from an observation simpler and more obvious than those just mentioned, concerning the difference of epic from drama: from the observation that Greek epic was recited, Greek tragedy enacted. Being unused to recited poetry, not to mention recited epic, we fail to imagine such experience; and meeting all Greek literature through the pallor of the text – generally the translated text - we fail to reimagine the vitality of all ancient Greek literary experience. The actual, physical presence of the living body in Greek tragedy made a life-challenging demand on its spectator which epic cannot have made. All we know of the historical-social background of Greek literature, indicates that tragedy fulfilled a more decisive existential function in Greek life than epic did. Epic served many functions, even – in the fifth-century – pedagogy. But epic was always more explicitly aimed at pleasing, as distinct from instructing, than tragedy was. Whether in feudal lords' halls or at Panionic festivals, the epic pleased an adventure loving people, whereas tragedy was charged with news about the human condition.

> 'And I wish that I were not any part
> of the fifth generation
> of men, but had died before it came,
> or been born afterward.'
> (*Works and Days*)

Chapter VI

Hesiod's Transitional Version of Epic Demand

Hesiod was born into a culture which – unlike Homer's – was groping toward the realization of democratic individualism. His culture was breaking hard but painfully from the world in which Homer lived.[1] The eighth century in Boeotia has been called a 'middle-age.' Political responsibility was still in the hands of a landholding nobility, *basileis* as Hesiod calls them. Those men administered justice and fought wars. But at the same time there was a growingly effectual feeling, among the peasantry and the nascent industrial classes, that power should be distributed. Hesiod calls the nobles 'gift-eaters,' for instance, and in the *Works and Days* frequently alludes to their irresponsibility. But discontent with the nobility was not the only source of social ferment. There was at the same time a growing and widespread awareness of the absolute importance of the individual. This awareness can easily be read out of Hesiod's own text. He discusses the peasantry as though each member of it had a duty, to his own soul, which took precedence over his duty to political superiors. Justice is a principle which absolutely coerces the farmer, while society can only coerce him relatively. Hesiod's attempt to relate the daily life of the common people to transcendent ethical principles – Dike, Themis, the order-pervaded world of Zeus – is the deepest unity between the *Works and Days* and the *Theogony,* his own two greatest works.

1. The question of the emergent spiritual forces of Hesiod's milieu has been discussed often. For a good general discussion of that milieu, cf. Schmid-Stählin, *Gesch. d. gr. Lit.,* 1, 1, 246-50. Cf. also Rzach, R. E., s.v. "Hesiod," 1176. There is a probing study of Hesiod in his age by Erich Voegelin, *The World of the Polis* (Baton Rouge, 1957) 126-64. He is concerned with Hesiod's, and his age's, break with the supposed anti-rational, mythical world of Homer. Voegelin's ideas should be read with skeptical interest.

In light of all this it is no surprise to find a strongly didactic and moralistic strain in Hesiod's poetry. Ethically-centered cultures naturally impose their basic concerns on contemporary writers: we can think of Cato the Elder, of Benjamin Franklin or Alexander Solzhenitzyn, and of the cultures around them. It could be further expected that Hesiod, as an artist, would have had trouble reconciling art and didacticism. The *dulce* and the *utile* are never that easily combined; especially when, as in the case of Hesiod, the inherited medium of expression is a highly refined, 'artificial' verse-form; when the inherited art-tradition is highly stylized. In fact Hesiod had such difficulty in harmonizing art with morality, that he stumbles in the effort, and in this stumbling shows his real nature and dilemma.

In working out that dilemma he takes us into an art-world which is far different from Homer's, yet which shares, with Homer's old epic world, much of its distance and objectification; much of that which seems to mark the epic genre. In our general contrast of epic with dramatic demands, we find Hesiod in the epic camp. We find him breaking from it to the degree he emerges as a person, in his work, to instruct the reader. But the result of that emergence is very different from what in Greek tragedy we were calling 'existential demand.' The demand of Hesiod's epic is more like, though still quite unlike, the personal demands made by the writers of Greek lyric.

i

After an invocation, the *Works and Days* opens with a picture of two kinds of Eris, Strife, one of which drives men to evil, while the other encourages them to profitable competition. Perses is then urged to be industrious — to feel the spur of the good Eris — and to lead a simple, honest life, far from the bribe-hungry nobles. There follows the line (42):[2]

> For the gods have hidden and keep hidden what could be men's livelihood.

> (Trans. of Hesiod by Richmond Lattimore)

2. All line references are to the Greek text in *Hesiod,* trans. Evelyn-White (London, 1929). I have been greatly helped by the elaborate notes in T. A. Sinclair's edition of the *Works and Days* (London, 1932).

Then Hesiod breaks into three tales: of Prometheus and Pandora, of the five ages, and of the hawk and the nightingale. They are meant as commentaries on line 42, and occupy the next 180 lines.

These three tales are explanations of Zeus' refusal to make life easy for men. In different, and superficially contradictory ways, the tales show man's responsibility for the evil condition in which Zeus has temporarily left him. The tales have a moral point. Yet they are not – perhaps with the exception of the third – 'moralistic.' They are aesthetically rich, deal richly with ideas through implication. In telling these stories, though, Hesiod faces a technical problem. Since the stories are thematically unrelated he needs to create verbal bridges into them, between them, and out of them. His manner of solving this problem interests me here.

The Prometheus myth opens (42 -48):

> For the gods have hidden and keep hidden
> what could be men's livelihood.
> It could have been that easily
> in one day you could work out
> enough to keep you for a year,
> with no more working.
> Soon you could have hung up your steering oar
> in the smoke of the fireplace,
> and the work the oxen and patient mules do
> would be abolished.
> But Zeus in the anger of his heart hid it away
> because the devious-minded Prometheus had cheated him.

There are two surprises. There is a sudden transition, in the first line of the passage, and then again in the line starting 'but Zeus . . .,' from the mundane to the transcendent world. In such flashes we grasp how close together those two worlds were in Hesiod's imagination. But there is a more typically Hesiodic surprise in the lines; the transition from direct address, aimed at Perses (43 -46), to a third-person narrative style (47 ff.). With line 47 the story begins. Such changes of direction or intention, especially as a transition to or from a story, are frequent and meaningful in Hesiod's poetry. Sometimes they call the addressed person's attention to the story. At other times they enable the author to express his own opinion. It is worth looking at three further examples of comparable transitions, taken from the tales with which the *Works and Days* opens.

At the end of the Prometheus-Pandora tale Hesiod steps out of the role of narrating mythologist – 'but the woman with her hands. . .' (94), 'Hope was the only spirit that stayed there. . .' (96) – in order to describe present troubles, stating that 'there are sicknesses that come to men by day, while in the night. . .' (102 -3). Then we are back abruptly with the second person singular (106 -7):

> Or if you will, I will outline it for you
>> in a different story,
> Well and knowledgeably – store it up
>> in your understanding – . . . . .

Perses' full attention is summoned.

After discussing the first four ages of the world Hesiod says that Zeus made a fifth generation. For the description of the earlier ages Hesiod had restricted himself to an historical style in the third person. Suddenly he writes (174 -75):

> And I wish that I were not any part
>> of the fifth generation
> of men, but had died before it came,
>> or been born afterward.

Then he goes on, as contemporary historian, to describe the iron age.

A final example of the point can be found at the end of the story of the iron age. The departure of Aidos and Nemesis has been apocalyptically prophesied (199 -200). Then there follows (202):

> Now I will tell you a fable for the barons,
>> they understand it.

This time it is the nobles, not Perses, who are addressed.

All of these examples illustrate a counterpoint between narrative mythical statement, projected at considerable aesthetic distance from the author, and abrupt personal intervention. To put it generically, we swing between the genuine epic and the nascent lyric world. The objectivity is briefly and sporadically punctured by the subject. The narrations, while presumably intended for Perses and the kings, actually speak to and presuppose a neutral, universal audience. On the other hand Hesiod's interventions – practically interruptions of himself – are more or less directly thrust at Perses or the kings, and at the same time forge rather rough links in the development of the poetry. The narratives are implication-full, stories with meaning. They have intellectual content without bald declaration of ideas. But the interventions in various ways establish a moralistic attitude toward the enframed stories. They surround them with content. At one time Hesiod will express his own attitude in these interventions, at another time he will urge Perses or the kings to watch out. In either case Hesiod's moralizing self is taking advantage of the necessary transitions in his narration, and punctuating them with admonitions.

ii

This admonitory manner — which emerges from but slowly subverts the epic manner — also expresses itself on more comprehensive levels of Hesiod's poetry. The inhabitants of the transcendent world which frames the events of the *Theogony*[3] are of three sorts: natural forces, like Chaos, Ocean, and Earth; the standard Olympian pantheon found in Homer; and what are generally considered abstractions, embodiments of ideas rather than personifications. In this last group I think first of Night, whose genealogy is related in lines 214-32 of the *Theogony*. Those offspring include, among others, Death, Blame, Woe, Nemesis, Deceit, Age, Strife, Toil, Forgetfulness, Famine, Sorrow, Fightings, Battles, Murders, Manslaughters, Quarrels, Lying Words, Disputes, Lawlessness, Ruin. Some of these offspring — Deceit, Lawlessness, or Lying Words — are what we could call forces of Evil, that is moral corruption, while others — Age, Toil, or Sorrow — are familiar plagues of human existence.

Friedrich Solmsen believes that these 'deities' are original with Hesiod,[4] and finds it puzzling that Hesiod includes them in this pantheon. They clash with the religious genius of Hellenism, which is hostile to abstract divinity, and characteristically anthropomorphic. One explanation for Hesiod's inclusion could be that the existence of these gods was from his ethical viewpoint a necessity, even though

3. Cf. Friedrich Solmsen, *Hesiod and Aeschylus* (Ithaca, 1949) for detailed and vital discussions of Hesiod's cosmogony. One of Solmsen's merits is to scrutizine the always significant minor deities in Hesiod. He leaves no important aspect of Hesiod unanalyzed in his study, and he draws a vast amount of secondary material into his scope.

4. Solmsen, pp. 28-31. There is a good remark on such deities in E. Bethe, *Die griechische Dichtung* (Wildpark-Potsdam, 1924) 61, where he is contrasting the sensuousness of an Archilochus to the tendency toward abstraction in parts of Hesiod's work. He writes: "so steht ihm (Hesiod) der epische Stil auch in dem Mahngedicht gut. Er geht immer ins Allgemeine und da er Begriffe noch nicht fassen kann, werden sie ihm Göttergestalten. . ."

aesthetically they may appear as little more than pale principles. Being a moralist, Hesiod saw reality as above all a battle-ground of ethical principles. Not only was he aware of goodness – though he says little about it – but he saw and described the moral negation of life around him. He saw both moral corruption and the recurrent plagues of the human condition. And, as is evident in the *Works and Days,* he considered the two things interrelated. In the story of Prometheus he observes that it was man's own evil – symbolized by the crime of the proud humanist – that was responsible for the creation of Pandora, and for the releasing of hardships and plagues into the world. Or, in the story of the flourishing of the just city and the ruin of the unjust one (*Works and Days,* 225 -37), it is clear that he considers the behavior of a society responsible for its happiness or misery. Evil and hardships seemed to him to be persistent and related features of human existence, and we can assume that he deified them because they were lasting features of reality. As a moralist Hesiod was determined to make a place for evil and hardships, as well as for growing justice, in his account of the structure of reality. He broke, as shaping poet, through even that veil of epic expression.

But the inclusion of evil forces in heaven is dangerous for a moralist, and Hesiod knew that. He leaves us, quite reasonably, with the possibility that if man could turn just all these evil principles would vanish from the pantheon, and another Golden Age would reappear on earth. The disastrous children of Night might disappear as in effect, Ouranos and Kronos have disappeared from Hesiod's pantheon by the time Zeus begins his reign. They have an historical but not an ontological presence, at that time. Thus Hesiod does not put the children of Night into his genealogy simply because of a desire to account for all that exists. That is only part of his intention. Nor does he include them only to lament their existence, for after all they are divine, that is, they *are,* in the deepest sense. Rather, as a good moralist, Hesiod combines these motives. He wants to account for all phenomena that are right or wrong, ethically speaking, but he also wants to leave no doubt of his belief that wrong should and can last no longer than necessary.

Hesiod's grounds for including the children of Night in his genealogy of the gods are basically moralistic. Many other examples could be chosen to show his ethical bias following him directly into the making of genealogy. But none would have proven the point as well as the present example. It shows Hesiod's determination to use the raw materials of Hellenic mythology, with its largely aesthetic character, as the foundation for an ethical argument. In other terms it shows him viewing the epically objective from a subjective angle.

iii

Turning from genealogy to story it is worth seeing how Hesiod deals with the core-story of the *Theogony,* the battle between Zeus, with his allies the Hundred-handed Giants, and the Titans. This *Titanomachia* permanently establishes Zeus' power, and completes the series of revolutions in heaven which have disposed of Ouranos and Kronos. Once the Titans are defeated Zeus is free to create, and to raise, a family of forces of order; Dike, Eunomia, the Muses, and many others. The struggle with the Titans is a symbolic one, in which Hesiod is telling us how order entered the universe, and raw might was destroyed.

The problem he faced, in describing this extended battle (617 -735), was to dramatize enlightened Zeus' victory over the hostile Titans, with the help of assistants who were quite as savage as the Titans but had joined Zeus. If Hesiod could have achieved that dramatization, he would have fused the vision of the artist with that of the moralist.

However the divinities in this drama have little personality. (So that we see here, again, how little dramatic this later epic work was.) In their speeches Zeus and Kottos express similar sentiments, clustered about two ideas: that Zeus has rescued the Hundred-handed ones from bitter slavery, and that they must fight for him out of gratitude. All this time the Titans are simply undescribed, blind forces who join in the cataclysmic fight. They seem no more evil than the Hekatoncheires. We only feel their presence, but never see them. In fact, we entirely miss here Homer's gift for conjuring up the character of a god in a few words. Hesiod seems not even to envy that gift. Yet the fact is that he is dealing with anthropomorphic gods, which are denatured as soon as they are treated as forces or principles rather than as projections of human beings.

The actual battle which Hesiod describes (654 -725) is potent and authentic, one of his greatest visions. But its development has strangely little to do with its outcome. The battle rages, the thunder crashes, the seas roar, and great courage is shown on both sides: meanwhile no sense of victory or defeat is given. There is complete deadlock, apparently, up to the unusual expression, 'the battle inclined,' *eklinthé de maché* (711). We read (711 -19):

> Then the battle turned; before that, both sides attacking
> in the fury of their rage fought on through the strong encounters.
> But now the three, Kottos and Briareos and Gyes,
> insatiate of battle, stirred
> the grim fighting in the foremost,
> for from their powerful hands they volleyed
> three hundred boulders
> one after another, and their missile flight
> overwhelmed the Titans
> in darkness, and these they drove
> underneath the wide-wayed
> earth, and fastened them there
> in painful bondage, for now they
> had beaten the Titan gods *with their hands*
> for all their high hearts.

Victory occurs suddenly, without our being given any sense of progressive conquest. (Contrast with this the feeling of surging and retreating lines in Homer's battle descriptions.) Consequently in this passage action and the course of moral-meaning never coincide. They have to be plotted on different graphs. The main body of the fighting has no moral-dramatic quality, while the moral punch is reserved entirely for the last lines quoted.

There are at least two ways in which Hesiod has failed to fuse aesthetic and moral vision in the *Titanomachia*. We had better not say that his moral speculation damages his art at this point. It is a question, rather, of lack of correspondence between aesthetic technique and moral notion. The *Titanomachia* has grandeur, and Hesiod makes his point. But he fails to take advantage of the resources of art; a serious failure for an artist. For an artist dealing in objective epic material it is especially serious. Hesiod is paying the price for occupying an uncertain position in the epic tradition.

iv

It is worth dwelling on the deeper sense of the art-didacticism conflict, as we find it in the *Works and Days* and the *Theogony*.

What was the source of that conflict? Did Hesiod house two equally powerful, but warring *personae?* [5] Or was he so basically either a moralist or artist that the presence of the opposite spirit — the aesthetic or the moral — was often difficult for him to absorb, and to harmonize? How are we to understand Hesiod's basic viewpoint?

He was basically a moralist,[6] impatient with that in the epic tradition which most contented itself with an objectifying aesthetic surface. Surely he was discontent with much that was greatest in Homer. We can hardly doubt, thinking over the *Works and Days* and the *Theogony,* that the perspective is one of 'right-and-wrong' more than of 'beauty-and-ugliness.' The avoiding of extended tales — which were the core of Homeric epic — and of personal confession — which was the core of the lyric creation — left Hesiod little room for whole-hearted aesthetic efforts. At the same time the themes that he chose — the eventual evolution of righteousness in heaven, and the means to that evolution on earth[7] — inclined him to, and sprang from, a concern with the 'moral.' Still even here, sure as we feel of the basic quality of Hesiod's creation, a qualification is wanted. It can't be said that he was only incidentally an artist; that, for instance, he expressed himself in the hexameter only because he had no choice, because he was locked in one stage of a language's development. For he often wrote what seems to be good poetry — as in much of the *Titanomachia* — and for the most part seems well at

5. The scattered and unreliable, but voluminous, biographical evidence about Hesiod can be found in Rzach's article (R.E., "Hesiod") 1168-73. A biographical study of Hesiod, drawing very literately on evidence from his poetry, and available external evidence, can be found in A. R. Burn, *The World of Hesiod* (New York, 1937) 31 -81.

6. Of course this assertion is not new. It was well put, for instance, by Maurice Croiset, *Histoire de la littérature grecque* (Paris, 1910) 1, 458 -61. We have striven for originality, here, only in bringing this truism about Hesiod under closer scrutiny, by confronting it with the artistic texture of his work.

For a concise discussion of the history of didacticism, in terms of which Hesiod's particular brand of moralism can be placed, cf. Allan Gilbert, s.v. "Didacticism," in Shipley's *Dictionary of World Literature* (New York, 1953) 101 -3.

7. To my mind Werner Jaeger, in *Paideia,* 1, trans. Highet (New York 1939) 55 -73, has argued most convincingly for the unity of Hesiod's works. He insists on Δίκη as the leitmotif of Hesiod's thinking, and earns his right to state, p. 64, that "Both (of Hesiod's) works reflect one man's consistent world-picture." I have been particularly helped by Jaeger's treatment of this question.

home in the hexameter.[8] We reach the more intangible point that Hesiod's formulation of his ethic must have depended closely on his ability to articulate the Boeotian of his day, a dialect which bore at least a vital inter-relation to his epic language. In other words we cannot suppose that Hesiod's moral position developed from a linguistic or artistic vacuum. It was a position won initially from and through language.

What Hesiod wants to say – the residue of idea or message, to the extent it can be isolated – frequently finds itself well joined to the way he says it. Content, in the sense of moral vision, is generally made one with form, in the sense of the manner of expressing that vision. But when a discrepancy appears in Hesiod's work, between content and form, the emphasis will be found to lie on the former – on the moral point as it usually turns out to be. That moral point will then appear – as is rare in Greek literature – in salient isolation. But the reverse situation does not occur. Hesiod never permits himself to be carried forward by style. Even in his love of the musical, especially of catalogues of musical names,[9] care for completeness and piety wins out. To the extent that an authentic conflict enters the texture of Hesiod's work, disturbing that perfect balance of content and form toward which art strives, the conflict rises from a dominance of content over form. In literary-historical terms that means an uncomfortable dominance of the personal over that in the epic tradition which was most impersonal.

8. For a nice "appreciation" of Hesiod's artistry, even in such lesser, but probably authentic, pieces as the *Catalogue of Women,* cf. Richmond Lattimore's introduction to his translation of *Hesiod* (Ann Arbor, 1959). Lattimore's own translation, incidentally, excellently preserves the dense, poetic texture of the best sections of his original. Cf. also, for discerning remarks on the purely "artistic" achievement of the *Theogony,* Paul Mazon's introduction to his text of *Hésiode* (Paris, 1947) 29-30.

9. For close study of such a catalogue, cf. Bruno Snell, "Die Welt der Götter bei Hesiod," *La Notion du Divin depuis Homère jusqu'à Platon,* 1, in *Entretiens sur l'Antiquité Classique* (Vandoeuvres-Genève,1952) 97-117.

Chapter VII

Solon's Consciousness of Himself

It is hardly necessary to emphasize the point about Greek epic, in contrast to Greek tragedy, which emerges from the last two chapters. Essentially, epic 'objectifies.' This was the point with Homer, one which sufficed to make his demands seem clearly different from those made by tragedians. Homer's demand was for attention, more than for engagement. The tragedians entered lives differently. And in this general division Hesiod needed to be paired with Homer, and apart from the tragedians. The case of Hesiod was complex. He made 'moral' demands; but was also a persuader and charmer from the older objective world, dealing like Homer with mythical-moral material, toward which one should as audience be prepared to take a purely 'objective' stance, feeling its independent qualities and coercions.

Greek tragedy and Greek epic, therefore, in many ways stand at a significant distance from one another. Tragedy makes a more intimate demand than epic. I have called this demand 'existential.' In relation to both these genres there are several perspectives in which Greek lyric could be considered.

The lyric can be viewed in terms of a different kind of demand. This is in fact the chief interest I plan here to take in Greek lyric. But the notion of 'demand,' in this instance, should be rather particularly understood.

The lyric poet – whether in ancient Athens, Renaissance Florence, or modern Chicago – imposes on us by forcing us to take an interest in himself, in his self. This distinguishes his work sharply from that of the ancient epic or dramatic writer, both of whom work out from themselves into public material, and into de-individualizing literary traditions. Yet the distinction of lyric from the other genres is not quite that sharp, especially where the ancient lyric voice is concerned.

The interest which Solon and Sappho force us to take in them, as selves, is not quite the same as that demanded by Petrarch, Chénier, Hart Crane, or even Walt Whitman. Solon and Sappho demand less interest in their personal uniqueness, though through their work they do still disclose themselves as self-centered and centripetal. With great ease, and no intrusively abstract intentions, Solon and Sappho manage to let themselves and their perceptions speak into the generality of the human situation. This is what they require us to notice in the depths of themselves. The uniqueness of the individual is in them much less to be stressed than it would later be — and is in our time. Yet in the large picture *this* modern-ancient distinction is small. Solon and Sappho — unlike Homer and Sophocles — ask us above all to be interested in *them*. Naturally they demand this because their genres demand this. But genres are made by men, not vice versa. As they were, Solon and Sappho could only write as they did.

The demand of Greek lyric, then, is on the whole different from that of the other two genres. It emerges from the personal demands exerted by the makers of Greek lyric. Here, three poets will illustrate. In this first chapter I illustrate with Solon.

i

Solon is not deep or wise
For when the god gave noble gifts, he refused.
He cast his net on the catch, but
Astonished, failed to draw in the yield.
Not equal to it in either heart or mind.
If I could rule, getting enormous wealth,
Governing Athens if only a single day,
I would willingly be flayed for a wineskin,
And see my race wiped out. (Fragment 33)

(Translations of Solon mine, unless otherwise indicated)

Oúk ephú Solón bathýphron oúde boúleeís anér
ésthla gár theoú didóntos aútos oúk edéxató;
péribalón d'agran, agastheis oúk epęspaseń megá
díktyón, thymoú th'hamárte kaí phrenón aposphaleís;
éthelón gar kén kratésas, ploúton, áphthonón labón
kaí tyránneusás Athénon moúnon hémerán mián,
áskos hýsterón dedárthai kápitétriphthái genós.[1]

1. All references to the text of Solon are to Bergk, *Poetae Lyrici Graeci* II (Leipzig,1914). Solon's fragments are analyzed and translated in Ivan Linforth, *Solon the Athenian* (Berkeley, 1919). I have used Linforth's analyses, but my own translations.

Even at first reading we notice the careful prosody of this fragment. The forceful, insistent trochees advance with considerable purely aural excitement, as in the sound repetitions of *bouleeis aner* or *hemeran mian.* The tetrameter lines are long enough for the poet to create an aural 'atmosphere' carefully and progressively. From the outset Solon is skillful at involving us with the surface of his language. Historians have enjoyed slighting his poetry, preferring to consider him only as statesman. It is true that he wrote his laws in verse. But he wrote them well.

We are also impressed at once in these lines with the easy, uncontrived development of a verbal attitude. Such a calm assurance about the technique of developing a poem impresses us in most of the Greek lyric poets. Archilochus, Sappho, and Alcman all seem to be saying just what they mean to say, in just the way they mean to say it. Solon's poem, for instance, falls into two parts. In the first four lines we are given an attitude toward him. The first line is offered as plain, abrupt fact, though it shows fine aesthetic assurance, introducing the poem as a whole. The next three lines justify the first, explaining how Solon was not *bathyphron* or *bouleeis.* The second line of the poem moves slightly out of the plain-statement mode of the first, speaking darkly of *esthla* and of God. In the following two lines we are carried all the way to metaphor. Solon has become a fisher, so astonished by the excellence of a catch that he fails to draw in his net. We do not know what 'noble things' the god gave, or what the catch is, but we know, or are brought dramatically to feel, that Solon's lack of wit lay in being so dazed by some rare opportunity that he neglected to take advantage of it.[2] The plain statement of the first line has been partially clarified, put into a richer but at the same time vaguer context.

The next three lines form the conclusion of the poem. They begin with a shift to the first-person and ostensibly explain, from that new angle, what Solon failed to take advantage of, though the narrator makes his explanation by telling what he would have done in Solon's place: that is, the lines are still a commentary, though in a different light, on the first line of the poem. (How much more fully commentary is integrated here than in Hesiod.) As a ruler (*kratesas*) the narrator would have had certain opportunities which Solon – we

2. For a straightforward statement of Solon's opportunity and what he did with it, cf. the context in Plutarch's *Solon.*

are to assume – also had, but ignored: the narrator could have become rich (*plouton aphthonon labon*) and have been tyrant *(tyranneusas)*. The poem is sealed with a final line in which the narrator, the 'I' of the poem, shows obliquely just how much he would have given to have had the opportunity which Solon missed. It is worth seeing that the exact character of Solon's missed opportunity is kept interestingly vague throughout the poem. This is mere artfulness, not concealment. More important is the persistent recurrence, in different perspectives, of the theme set in the first line. The poem is strangely complex, yet simple and unified in mood. The 'I' of the last three lines is really just developing a single attitude in several ways.

The purely structural complexity of the poem shows itself to be much more than that when one considers that Solon wrote it, so that the critical narrator of the poem (who appears in *ethelon* or *labon*) can hardly – or cannot simply – be taken to impersonate Solon's own attitude. With another poet than Solon this last statement might be open to question. We might take the whole poem as self-ridicule. But this would simply not be in the spirit of Solon. It would be undercut by everything else we know about him. The whole poem, in fact, is the expression of an attitude toward Solon. That attitude, of course, is critical. It tries to put Solon in an absurd light, implying that he is stupid and hesitant. Yet the poem is finally not self-ridicule, because the 'I' in the poem very nicely discredits himself. The last three lines prove that. The last line, in fact, is such a violent expression of self-debasement, on the narrator's part, that it turns the poem into an attack against the narrator rather than into an instrument of self-criticism on Solon's part. The concealed attack is highly successful. Despite initial appearances to the contrary, the poem becomes a subtle vehicle for Solon's praise of himself on moral grounds.

Of particular interest, here, is the kind of self-consciousness which Solon shows in the poem he has written. It is chiefly through self-consciousness that he represents his inner life to us. In itself his verbal accomplishment, in putting an attitude toward himself into the mind of another, is significant. The development and expansion of the notion of the self was a gradual and difficult feat of early Greek experience. The attainment of self-consciousness required, for one thing, a realization which Solon attains artistically, by standing artificially outside of, and looking at, himself in this poem. To integrate such self-awareness into art is difficult.

This introduces a point which holds generally for the Greek poets in their quest for the self. They were not in search of an ineffable essence in themselves. Roughly speaking, they did not try to express the 'soul,' in anything like the post-classical sense of the word. They looked on themselves as parts of the natural world, and took it for granted that their experiences and attitudes were expressible in natural and accessible language.

ii

In the fragment considered above, Solon writes no *deep* awareness of his self: I stressed only his surprisingly 'objective' perception of himself as a distinct entity among other selves. This kind of perception does not set him apart from other Greek lyric poets, but, on the whole, it is rarer with most than with Solon.[3] Archilochus tells us a good deal about himself: what he loves, what he hates, how the senseworld strikes him. But in all this 'expression of himself' he integrates little awareness of his own self's distinct nature and position. This is what limits his self-consciousness: his self has not yet been brought into a system of defining relations. When he writes that

> By spear is kneaded the bread I eat,
> by spear my Ismaric wine is won,
> which I drink, leaning upon my spear,

(Trans. of Archilochus by Lattimore)

we feel we are learning a lot about the poet, and it is clear that he has here raised the physiognomy of his own nature into reason and form. Yet his statements emerge too directly *out of* the self to include any reflexive awareness of the self. This is generally true of Sappho and Alcman, also.[4]

---

3. Bruno Snell's *The Discovery of the Mind,* trans. Rosenmeyer (Cambridge, Mass., 1953) analyzes the discovery of the self, though only incidentally. The attempt to describe and evaluate the "spiritual" components of man is Snell's main theme. His arguments are often enlightening for the present question of the discovery of the self in literature. Cf. also, on the place of Solon in the development of Greek *Geistesgeschichte,* Schmid-Stählin, *Gesch. d. gr. Literatur* (Munich, 1929) I. 1, 368-71, and Friedrich Solmsen, *Hesiod and Aeschylus* (Ithaca, 1949) 107-23, where Solon's spiritual effort is stimulatingly placed relative to those of Hesiod and Aeschylus.

4. On this distinctive characteristic of Greek lyric poetry, cf. Werner Jaeger, *Paideia* I, trans. Highet (New York, 1939) 114 ff. I owe a great deal here to

With Solon the 'outer' conditions for such reflectivity were more favorable than with these other poets. In his youth he was an *homme d'affaires* and travelled through Ionia, visiting in highly cultivated court circles. He was from a good family and knew the best men of Athens. More importantly, he had from the time of his youth an interest in politics; becoming in middle age the archon of Athens, with exceptional powers. From this position he gave the Athenians new laws, new currency, and a new constitution. As archon he was continually called on to mediate between the aristocracy and the proletariat. This difficult life in the public eye, with the demands it made on his natural integrity and decency, no doubt forced him to a clearer awareness of himself, of his own nature, and of his intellectual 'position.' Caught between cross-fires of opposing viewpoints, he came to realize what he stood for, and therefore inevitably to have a better idea of what he was. In these circumstances, too, he can be contrasted with the majority of the remaining Greek lyric poets: with Archilochus the soldier, Sappho the lover, Alcman the emancipated slave.

These 'outer' conditions of Solon's self-awareness are certainly relevant here, for they are constantly integrated, as subjects as well as ingredients of attitudes, into his verse. I want to clarify this point by looking at three poems, starting with one of Solon's most famous elegies:

> To the common people I gave the strength they need,
> Neither retracting their honors nor tempting with more:
> Those who had power and position through wealth,
> Those too I was careful to shelter from indignity.
> I took my stance, casting a strong shield over both parties,
> And allowed neither to triumph unjustly.

Again (even in translation) we can sense the confident and skillful prosody. Solon has made the poem into the naturalness of a calm mind. But especially interesting for the present question is the way the form echoes his viewpoint. The poem is divided into three 'couplets,' each of them closed, as generally in the Greek elegy. The first couplet coincides with Solon's statement of just how much he gave to 'the people,' while the second couplet does the same for the statement about the aristocracy. In each case the talk of limited

Jaeger's discussion. His arguments gain in strength, it seems, for being part of an over-all vision of Greek culture.

giving is reinforced precisely by the formal limits of the poem. Just as the 'idea' of the final couplet unifies the 'ideas' of the first two couplets, so that last couplet appears as a kind of formal crown to the poem. The three distinct acts of Solon are marked off and 'formalized' by the structure of the poem.

Solon's image of 'casting a strong shield over both factions' is successful and clear, provided it is not pressed too closely into its sensuous details. Such pressure is not invited, because Solon's poetry is unusually nonsensuous, relying little, for example, on exact visual imagery. Thus we are ready to read such an image as this, of the shield, simply for its conceptual drift. That drift is clear. Solon saw himself as a strong, impartial leader, as he informs us in this poem, and as such he both unified – indeed, clamped down on – both factions of the city, and cast a symbol of protection, the shield, over both of them. In the casting of the shield, then, he tries to make it clear that he is not only a limit-prescriber for his society, but is also its unifier and protector. The poem develops a surprisingly complex attitude of Solon toward himself. It is characteristic of his mind that no trace of 'egotism' enters this attitude, no foolish or imprudent self-praise.

In another poem, written in iambic trimeters (frags. 36, 37), Solon expresses more dramatically this awareness of his self's political context. He relates the four good things he has done for Athens. He has freed the land from bondage (mortgages), has brought many Athenians back home, has freed many Athenians from slavery, and has given laws equally to the good and bad. In the fragment (37) which belongs to the end of that poem he says that if he had done what his opponents had wanted, the city would have lost many men. At the end we read:

> This was why I turned like a wolf in a dog pack
> Defending myself from attack on every side.

This time he has joined a clear, strong image to his forceful iambs, making a peculiarly final statement of his political troubles. In a way the visual objectivity, with which Solon here sees himself, reminds us of fragment 33. Sappho, expressing her love-consumed self, or Archilochus his passionate, brutal self, are rarely able to stand beyond those selves, are rarely able to assess their own natures with this clear Solonian eye. Seldom is Solon, for that matter, able to translate his self-awareness into visual terms.

As a final example I want to mention a fragment (32) in which Solon's theme is his distinctively ethical self.

> If I spared my fatherland
> And did not seize hold of tyranny and force,
> Polluting and shaming thereby my reputation,
> I am not ashamed. For I think that thus
> All the more I excel other men.

The 'I am not ashamed' is a potent understatement. It introduces, here, a direct statement of moral principle, in which Solon himself breaks out rather anti-poetically from the surface of his verse, and addresses us with an unaccustomed edifying voice. (As he is never egotistic, he is almost never moralistic.) He is assessing his political achievement, and asserting the unity of moral behavior with right political action. He asserts this not as an easy gnomic idea, but as a comment on his own experience in the political world. Even in the case of the clause 'all the more,' it is important to see what a conquest over ordinary language and ordinary sentiment has been won. In Solon's case, it appears to be won precisely by his attention to his own nature and its experiences.

iii

The evidence of Solon's self-awareness and self-presentation hardly goes farther than the few fragments assembled here. There are some 283 verses of Solon extant, and few of them concern the present question. I want to draw together a few observations suggested by the poems already discussed.

In his poetry, Solon did not seek for the self as an ineffable essence in him. In this he was like the other Greek lyric poets. In most of them 'expression of self' is only a hesitant step taken toward the discovery of the 'I.' Such 'expression' is different from 'reflection onto the self.' Solon is exceptional for his 'reflectiveness' in this sense. Even in *his* poetry, though, we see chiefly a reflection onto the public characteristics of the self, a preoccupation which was to be expected from so publicly oriented a man. In the fragments considered here, Solon has been looking back (in time as well as in 'space') on the events of his moral life: on its decisions, actions, and situations. He looks back as though from a great distance on these events, with an innate nobility of vision which Hermann Fränkel calls 'unfeierliches Pathos, das für seine Haltung und Dichtung be-

zeichnend ist.'[5] His self presents itself to him with none of the
immediacy of its 'accidents,' such accidents as sense-impressions. Nor
does it appear as a center or reason of aesthetic appreciation, although in its poetic incarnation it is translated aesthetically. His self
emerges, through the language in which he presents it, as a generative
core of his moral life. The moral argument in Hesiod was blurred,
projected far and obscuringly, as it turned out, into epic material. In
Solon the moral argument emerges directly, as an immediate result of
his negotiation with himself.

It remains to consider Solon's distinctive self-awareness in
relation to his whole (poetically expressed) vision of life. A single
example will suggest that relation and indicate the literary-historical
importance of Solon's self-consciousness. He is aware of his own self
as a center of moral events. It is no surprise, then, to find that he
looks on other selves as such centers. He continues the tradition, first
made evident among the Greeks in Hesiod, of calling upon the
individual to grow conscious of his moral responsibilities. We have
seen Hesiod doing this in the *Works and Days,* where, generalizing
from his own experience with an unjust brother, he clearly insisted
that Justice is a real principle, one which must be respected. Hesiod
had spoken in universal terms, convinced that justice is an obligation
falling equally on every man, king or peasant. Solon makes this same
projection from his own experience, insisting on the absolute wrong
of lawlessness and the absolute right of lawfulness. Both these
principles, he claims, present themselves to every individual, and
cannot be sidestepped. His awareness of his moral self is clearly
related to this insistence on the moral responsibility of every self.[6]

This appeal to the individual conscience is made with great
force in Solon's long poem *To the Athenians* (fragment 4). That
poem opens with a diatribe against the injustice of the leading,

5. Hermann Fränkel, *Dichtung und Philosophie des frühen Griechentums*
(New York, 1951) 292. Fränkel sees clearly into the characteristics of Solon's
verse and is willing, like Jaeger, to consider Solon primarily as a poet. Fränkel's
fidelity to the text itself generates his "realistic" aesthetic interpretation.

6. In addition to the important discussions of Solon's *Dike* and *eunomia* in
Solmsen (above, note 3), cf. Gregory Vlastos, "Solonian Justice," *CP* 41 (1946)
65 -83. That article considers *Dike* as a creative principle which works to join a
community of like-minded citizens. Vlastos documents his argument thoroughly
and develops it convincingly.

insatiable citizens, and culminates in the broad charge that they neglect Justice. For this, Justice brings slavery and strife into the city.

> Thus public calamity comes to each man's home,
> The gates of his courtyard are unwilling to guard him,
> Over the high gate calamity leaps, and finds him,
> Even though fleeing he waits in the innermost nook of his room.

The picture of the city haunted to its last nook by evil is one of the great visions of Greek poetry. This evil, which follows every man into his home, is the product of a discord in the state (*stasis*), which was caused by a few men. Individual evil, that is, can cause a flood of evil for a whole state. Solon emphasizes the moral responsibility of the individual in his community. In his elegy *To Himself* (fragment 13) he had emphasized the individual's responsibility to his descendants, or *genos*. Speaking of the man who is unjust-minded, he says:

> One man pays at once, another later. If
> The man himself escapes the fate of the gods,
> It comes most surely again; though blameless, the children
> Or later descendants will pay his penalty.[7]

In one way or another, the individual's moral behavior extends far beyond himself. For that reason, Solon is saying, the individual needs to know his moral self. This insistence seems to be related to his own self-awareness. It might even be said that Solon's self-consciousness is the ground for his belief in the importance of self-awareness in others. Simply stating this relationship reveals the importance of the context of Solon's self-awareness.

    If Solon's distinctive form of self-consciousness is connected with his consciousness of the 'situation' of the self in general, then his self-consciousness becomes an ingredient in his *historical* achievement. That achievement was many-sided, of course: he was a creative lawgiver, economic reformer, and politician – in the Greek sense – as well as a poet.[8] Still there was unity to his efforts. It lies in the

---

    7. Among the many discussions of this complex, oddly organized poem, I have been helped especially by C. M. Bowra, "Solon," *Early Greek Elegists* (Cambridge, Mass., 1938) 89-100, and by Richmond Lattimore, "The First Elegy of Solon," *AJP* 68 (1947) 161-79. I have attended mainly to less complex or ambitious poems of Solon in this chapter only because they are more relevant to my subject.

    8. For a thorough biographical-historical study of Solon, cf. Linforth (above,

conviction of the worth of the individual self's moral development. I don't suppose that Solon admired Justice on abstract grounds. He admired it for its power to bring into the state a harmonious situation in which each man could find his place and direction for growth. The same motive, no doubt, urged Solon to free the land from slavery, that is from mortgages which kept the majority of Athenians in debt, and therefore unable to develop themselves with moral self-respect. For the same reason, I guess, Solon opened the Ecclesia to the Thetes, and the judicial courts to everyone. It is important, of course, not to consider the Solon of these acts a committed democrat. In many ways he valued the traditional organization of society: as, say, in his admiration for rightfully inherited wealth. Yet he was a democrat to the extent that democracy means a collection of morally responsible, that is self-aware, individuals.

The consciousness of the importance of each moral self, on which Solon's historical achievement rests, may be related to his own self-consciousness. This point gives peculiar importance to the poetic fragments analyzed here. They permit us to see Solon dealing intimately with his own being, and in a manner unique among Greek lyric poets. His self-consciousness is distinctively moral and radiates a demand onto moral self-consciousness in other men. It shows how immediately demanding lyric poetry could make the ethical concerns which in epic were muted, and which in tragedy were expressed through an entirely different, oblique and participatory, channelling of sensibilities.

note 1) 3-102. His study is very careful, bringing out the details of Solon's activities only to the degree that ascertainable facts permit, preferring prudence to imagination when the choice arises. Kathleen Freeman, *The Work and Life of Solon* (Cardiff, 1926), supplies many details on Solon's constitutional innovations.

'Hither to me from Crete
To this holy temple
Where you will find your lovely grove of apples,
    And your altars perfumed with frankincense.'
(Sappho, fragment 2)

Chapter VIII

Sappho and Poetic Motion

It is possible to view the lyric as a fairly direct effort to 'objectify' or 'project' the inner life. But as is clear in the case of Solon, such 'projection' is only possible in terms of the rules of language, and of one's introspective relation to himself. The lyric demand may be far more immediate than the epic — Solon's than Hesiod's — but it is only immediate in the way permitted by literature. Greek lyric is only as free as Greek literature permits it to be. Solon was not free, psychologically or metaphysically speaking, to 'pour himself forth' into his verse. Of course this restriction applied even more to the epic writers. Homer worked through and into a 'subjectivity-muting' tradition. Hesiod did so equally, despite his restlessness with the epic stance. The question of rules of language, of linguistic limitations upon pure self-expression, is in all these writers no less important than that of tradition-made psychological limitations: ultimately the two questions are closely related. The rules of language, including not only the 'laws' of grammar but the body of tropes and verbal habits which constitute literary tradition, are deeply involved with the laws or limitations of the inner life, itself only developing and ripening in terms of language. What must be projected is already unconsciously verbalized. Has the lyric poet, then, any inward life which is to some degree independent of langugage, and which he can project? How closely do language and subjectivity, in this case, amount to the same thing? Answering this, even in part, will help us to appreciate the ancient lyric demand.

I will content myself, in answer to the complex question, with the notion that in the lyric poet there are certain dramatic tendencies which seek expression in words.[1] The points about Solon will thus

1. It is worth seeing that such tendencies are not solely part of the study of psychoanalysis, even of the psychoanalysis of the "literary" mind. They are

be put in other terms. One form the lyric poet's dramatic tendencies adopt is that of motion toward, away from, and of different kinds. There is a kind of inner kinesis in the psyche. What is important about this *kinesis,* what forms its *raison d'être,* is its power to dramatize certain attitudes, or constellations of feelings. Thus the inner drama of motion 'upward' will often be associated with the notion (or attitude) of spiritual ascension, and that of motion 'downward' with the notion of spiritual descent, corruption, etc. It is obvious – but still worth saying – that the association between such felt inner patterns of movement, and actual spiritual conditions, the 'objectively' psychological, is purely imaginary. Such an association has no grounding in 'physical' reality. Motion upward has nothing real to do with spirituality. And so on. Yet the kind of association involved here is a fact of the utmost importance both in ordinary language and in 'literary' language. Here I look to the way Sappho, in her verse, manipulates a pair of these kinetic forces, thus exercising what for her was a characteristic inner demand.

i

Motion 'toward' or 'away from' the presenter of the poem is of continual importance in the largely fragmentary remains of Sappho. (As a theme in her poetry it occupies the place played, in Solon's poetry, by spiritual movement in toward the poet as subject). This pattern has a fundamental connection with Sappho's erotic temperament. More of that soon. First we can notice a single famous example of *stasis,* arrested motion, in her verse, and then work out from that point. In fragment 31 (1-4) we read:

> Beyond all heavenly fortune seems to me
> the man who sits facing you and listens
> intimately to your sweet speech. . .

(Trans. of Sappho by P.M.Hill unless otherwise indicated).

The nearness of 'the man' (*kenos*) to Sappho's beloved is doubly emphasized by the use of both 'facing' (*enantios*) and 'near' (*plasion*) to describe his location. The emphasis fits with the poet's double

concerned also with "inner geometry." Such works as G. Bachelard's *L'eau et les rêves* (Paris, 1956) or Maud Bodkin's *Archetypal patterns in poetry* (Oxford, 1951) are studies which approach in method, and on a far larger scale, the kind of inquiry sketched here.

intention: to express jealousy of the 'nearness' of 'that man' to the beloved; and to contrast 'the man's' presumed ability to endure such radiant presence, with Sappho's own debility in that presence. 'The man's' 'location,' under the circumstances, is significant.

Sappho frequently links the amatory mood, founded by such a treatment of 'location', with motion toward the presumed presenter of the poem. Often such motion is put into the form of a 'conventional' supplication of divinity, usually of Aphrodite. (*Supposed* conventionality: after all the tradition was to call upon divinity or the Muse, as Homer did, to *speak*, not to approach). Thus in fragment 1, addressing Aphrodite, Sappho says (5 -7):

> But come to me, if ever in the past, at other times,
>> You hearkened to my songs,
>> And harnessed the golden chariot, and left
>> Your father's house and came to me.

It becomes clear in this poem that Sappho *really* wants the goddess to come, as the goddess has done before. Lines 9 -13 are in fact devoted to fanciful, but – in the poetic context – quite real former descents of Aphrodite to Sappho. A tangible sense is created here that the poet is inviting real presence to come near her. This sense is reinforced by a return to the invitation at the end of the poem. Sappho says (25 - 26):

> So come to me now, release me from grievous care. . .

and, at the last (28):

> And be my ally.

Goddess stand by my side, the poet says.

In another poem (fragment 2) Sappho makes such an invitation – also to Aphrodite – even more tangible. We are here far from the verbal world in which the poet simply wants 'inspiration' from the Muse. The actual presence of Aphrodite, always in terms of literary illusion, is invited with a variety of sensuous details which makes the mood of approach and nearness unmistakeable.

> Hither to me from Crete
> To this holy temple
> Where you will find your lovely grove of apples,
> And your altars perfumed with frankincense.

> (My translation)

And so on, with description of the water, branches, roses, leaves, which make a seductive bower of the place to which Aphrodite is being invited.[2] The notion of seduction, in fact, is in place here. Particularly – or is this to confuse the 'divine' with the human? – when we consider Sappho's own homosexuality, such an invitation to Aphrodite seems erotically tinged. At the end of the poem (13 -16) it appears that Aphrodite is wanted chiefly to perfect some mood of festivity, a nectar-heavy mood. But it is almost as though the goddess would *be* the perfection of that mood. She will be no mere Ganymede, trotting with her chalice from cup to cup.

Finally, to turn to an example of verbalized approach which exists on a more 'objectified' plane, there is the description of the wedding of Hector and Andromache (fragment 44). Here the poet is not calling the wedding assembly *toward* her; she describes the movement of the newly married pair toward Troy, and their joyous reception in the city. Yet though the poem is badly mutilated it is still suffused with a strong sense of 'arrival.' While projecting the entire situation into unlocalized objectivity, Sappho has in feeling miraculously taken the place of a Trojan woman welcoming home her leader and his bride. As she describes the sound of cymbals, the holy songs sung, the smell of incense in the streets, we have a sense of being there, of witnessing the 'coming.' Characteristically of Sappho – though also part of the exigency of the subject – we are made almost insensibly aware of the place *toward which* motion is taking place, though we are much less aware of the motion itself.

Motion 'away from' a set point is, by contrast, a less important dramatic theme in Sappho's verse. She easily conceives her language around the axis of departures and absences, but cannot so readily dramatize the feeling of 'motion from' as of 'motion toward.' In fragment 1 a brief passage of great technical refinement brings both axes of Sappho's inner drama together, and introduces the point. Aphrodite is imagined having asked Sappho, formerly, how she can help her to win over a reluctant lover. The goddess inquires (19 -24):

> And whom must I now bend to your love –
> Who is it, Sappho, who has wronged you?
> For even if she flees you, quickly will she pursue you,
> And if she now refuses gifts, tomorrow she will give them;

2. Sappho, like other Greek lyric poets, was not chiefly interested in nature as a setting for dialogue between poet and divinity. Cf., for excellent remarks on the "settings" of Sappho's lyrics, Max Treu, *Sappho* (Munich, 1958) 137-42.

> Yes, and if she loves you not to-day soon will she love you, despite
> herself.

Concisely, Sappho expresses the whole dialectic of her inner life. Departure from and motion toward an established point — the poet herself — are both dramatized. The interaction of the poles is made peculiarly tight through the embodiment in a single person, Sappho's beloved, of both forms of motion. Now she is fleeing, tomorrow she will pursue.

In two other significant fragments of Sappho we find the notion of parting clearly emphasized, and with it, though not explicitly described, a sense of 'motion away' from the poet. Fragment 96 is addressed to Atthis, to console her for the loss of a girl who has gone to Lydia:

> . . .how especially she loved your singing.
> And now among the Lydian women she shines. . .

The bulk of the remaining poem is concerned with a simile, comparing the absent girl to the moon, which is pre-eminent among the stars and shines placidly down on the peaceful world. The force of the whole is to emphasize the beautiful *distance* of the absent girl. Only in the lines quoted above is her departure felt; the rest of the poem makes the *loss* tangible.

Fragment 94 presents a dialogue between Sappho and a friend who has left her. The introduction to the dialogue is this:

> . . .she wept bitterly when she left me and said to me. . .

Most of the remaining poem, then, consists of Sappho's effort to console her friend — as she had consoled Atthis (fragment 96) — for the parting. The consolation takes the form of a list of pleasures formerly shared by the two lovers. And yet, as we see in the beginning line of the poem,

> . . .I wish in truth that I were dead,

Sappho is herself not consoled. As Denys Page says, about this line:

> . . .that was not said at the time of parting; it is what she says now, when she recalls the scene of parting and all that it means to her. At the time, she played the part of the stronger spirit, the comforter, in the presence of her distraught companion; today she avows a grief as great as her companion's or greater. [3]

---

3. *Sappho and Alcaeus* (Oxford, 1955), 82.

It can be asked whether anything deeper is noticed here in Sappho than selected instants in her highly emotional existence. Isn't it simply that she, living in the sophisticated and relatively cosmopolitan society of 6th century Lesbos, was continually subject to comings and goings, and has recorded that experience in her poetry? As Page writes:

> They (these girls) come from Miletus, from Phocaea, from Colophon, to live in Sappho's society; and one day they go away again.[4]

As we know, however, poetry is always only a more or less indirect record of lived life. In the present case we could insist that Sappho's invocation-poems — those in which she invites the presence of Aphrodite or Hera — have no factual reality. Nor do they seem to be merely conventional. They are not simply Muse-inviting poems. Rather they correspond to some inner 'intention' of the author. In the same way the dialectical treatment of pursuit and flight in fragment 1, discussed above, is clearly witty, part more of a conceit than of a confession. Or the time-lag device of fragment 94, which contributed to the poignancy of that poem, was a transparently successful concession to artifice. In other words, it will do much less than complete justice to Sappho's poems to think of them as auto-biographical records. The demand for attention to self, in the Greek lyric, does not express itself *that* directly.

I suggest that part of what we find in the pitifully small remainder of Sappho is the record of a strong, almost geometrical, inward 'concern' with patterns of coming and going. It cannot be said that the comings and goings in her verse are autobiographically explicable; though many of them probably are. Nor, at the opposite extreme, do those comings and goings express almost abstractly inward tensions, without much vital content. The truth lies somewhere between. Sappho is inwardly disposed to experiences which fall into patterns of coming and departure. This inward disposition doubtless had roots in some ultimate erotic tendencies, such as those of inviting the world to her breast, and of dreading the trauma of losing the world. And those very roots were tangled with her society and its values. But we can only go so far, here, into such a tangle. At

4. *Ibid.*, 95.

the least Sappho's inward and deep disposition readied her to find suitable for her poetry such experiences, in all their vitality, as she has there embodied. In a sense she only experienced, and offered us, what she was.

'She held a branch of myrtle and
Flowering rose and down her back
And shoulders flowed her hair.'

(Archilochus, fragment 29)

Chapter IX

Archilochus and his Senses

A word of qualification.

The inroads of the artist's personality into his work can begin to be traced in Hesiod. He does not reveal his inner life through character-creation, since he is a didactic, not a narrative, epic writer. Rather in him we begin to sense a small change in the whole cast of the work, a suffusion of the literary whole with its maker's selfhood. No one will think, of course, that Homer was absent from *his* work, that he was simply the selfless voice of the early Greek people. The demands of the epic genre are not severe in that way. Nor are Homer's characters, Achilles or Odysseus, thin projections of inner life. They are anything but that. Homer was in touch with the secret of personality. We could say, in turning to the slightly new traits in Hesiod, and then to the outburst of lyric poetry, that a more intimate, and far more direct, entry of the artist's self into his work is apparent, an entry far less obliquely masked than in Hesiod. We don't want to say that Greek lyric is a direct reflection of its maker, even that it is an autobiographical document. That confusion, in its turn, would show little acquaintance with the obliqueness of all literature. In the present chapter, I will necessarily speak of what Archilochus feels and thinks, as it reveals itself in his poetry; but this is simply the needed shorthand for a more complex idea: that Archilochus – like Solon and Sappho – chose to project his own inner life into a certain kind of transfiguring and enriching verbal Gestalt. All three writers come close to us with the existential urgings of their work, perhaps more immediately close than any other Greek writers. But each of their immediacies remains touched with artifice.

i

The immediacy of Archilochus' sense-experience to his poetry strikes us first in meter. It is hard to feel, with Homer or Hesiod, that the lived texture of the poet's experience is directly translating itself into the sound of his verse.[1] We can hardly feel this with the tragedians; rarely even in their choral odes. But in Archilochus patterns of sound convey sensuous experiential overtones more directly even than does meaning. Nor, in this case, is such a distinction of sound from meaning simply academic. In Archilochus' poetry, where sound and meaning are united, we can concentrate on one of those two elements to the exclusion of the other. Concentration on sound patterns is especially worth while when it comes to Greek poetry, because of the attention the Greek poets gave to their prosody.

It is significant that Archilochus expressed himself through sensuous, heavily rhythmic, quickly oscillating meters.[2] The ancient Greeks, who admired Archilochus most among their lyric poets, considered him the inventor of the iamb, thus of one of the most 'heavily sensuous' Greek meters. It is true that he is the first extant Greek poet to offer us this meter. He used it especially in his satires (the verb *iambo* means 'to assail') where it seemed to copy the contours of his caustic feelings. For example (fragment 31):

Old woman that she was, she failed to bathe.

(Trans. of Archilochus mine unless otherwise indicated).

Or (fragment 33):

An awful racket roamed the house.

(kat' oikon eśtrophato dýsmeneś babaks).

This is also the meter of many of his erotic poems, where aural sensuousness duplicates sensuous meaning. In those erotic poems Archilochus frequently combines trochees with iambs, letting the two meters vacillate in a powerful counterpoint. Even the trochee is sensuous, as he manipulates it. Occasionally, as in some of his tetrameters, he writes purely trochaic verse. Fragment 50 reads:

Homeless, fellow-citizens, now grasp my words. . .

(ó lipérnetés polítai, táma dé ksyníeté / hrémat).

1. For a recent effort both to date all these writers, and to characterize their rapidly changing social environment, cf. A. R. Burn, *The Lyric Age of Greece* (New York, 1960).
2. For general discussions of Archilochus' prosody, cf. Amédée Hauvette, *Archiloque* (Paris,1905)132 -162;and, more recently, the treatment in *Archiloque: fragments* (Paris,1958) lxii -lxix, by François Lasserre.

Or (fragment 52):

> So the wretchedness of all the Greeks had come to Thasos. . .

> (Hós Panéllenoń oídzys és Thasón synédramén)

Both of Archilochus' chief meters rely on abrupt and sensuous rhythmic emphases. (By contrast, say, with the epic dactyl, which is more monotonous, less tense). These few examples must do for evidence.

In judging the sensuous qualities of the iamb and the trochee in Archilochus, and the way those meters are revelatory, it is useful to remember the social context of the production of that verse: that, like Homer's and Pindar's, it was often recited publicly and to musical accompaniment. The way in which Archilochus composed his verse is open to question: no doubt he could write, living as he did in the first half of the seventh century, but did he compose by singing? He does speak of reciting to the flute (Fragments 123, 76). That alone proves that as creator he must have been highly conscious of the pitch and key of his prosody, as well as of its simpler stress pattern. It is also certain that in public recitations his verse was recited to the flute and the lyre. He turned directly to his audience. On such occasions his poetry may have sounded more like musical recitative than like poetry as we know it. Yet the innate sensuousness of his meter, as we read it now, must have been created *into* an originally all-embracing sensuous context. We are required, here, to make the same effort as in assessing the overall sensuous creation of the Greek temple, with its organic inter-functioning of shape, medium, and color.

The effort to appreciate the immediate sensuous context of Archilochus' verse is not enough: we must also look into the sensuous-historical background of that verse. We should remember that although Archilochus was the *literary* founder of the iamb, and although he is the first *extant* Greek poet to offer us trochees, there was for both meters a communal choral-religious origin which reached far into the past which preceded Archilochus. For one thing, the exchanging of insults and obscenities in iambic meter was an approved part of early Greek religious ceremonies.[3] But there is a

---

3. Cf. Hauvette, *op. cit.*, 140 ff. The social-religious origins of the lampooning iambic spirit, as well as of the verse-form itself, are taken up by Werner Jaeger, *Paideia* I (trans. Highet, New York, 1939), 119-121. He

further explanation for the early use of those meters. Iambs and trochees are both appropriate to rapid dances. (Dactyls are not). It is assumed that dances in those meters took place in festivals of Demeter and Dionysus, that is in religious fertility ceremonies. The name *ithyphallic*, given to one of the oldest trochaic forms, points to this origin. There is a passage in Aristophanes' *Frogs* (383 ff.) in which a rural celebration of Demeter is recited in hopping iambic dimeters, in the way we can well imagine it was recited long before Archilochus. The sensuousness of these meters in Archilochus, then, has a sensuous-historical context. Yet surely these meters rise directly from inside Archilochus, not from his subservience to tradition. He used the tradition because it suited his aesthetic needs. His inner sense-experiences found appropriate form in such meters.

ii

Discussion of meter is particularly dangerous; it appeals to untestable subjective responses. We can turn to the question of the kind of experience Archilochus seems to embody in meter; to the experiential content of his poetry. It is a truism that the lyric is an expression of the self. But so, in a sense, is even the Homeric epic. We have already been through some of the complexities of this issue of self-expression. The Homeric epic is a very oblique expression of the self, one conditioned by powerful 'external' factors, such as verbal traditions or inherited stories. While even the ancient lyric, in distinction to the later romantic lyric, was seriously bound by 'external' conditions. That ancient lyric must be seen in the context of the whole Greek poetic achievement. Archilochus, for example, made no effort to 'express himself,' or at least to do what we often understand by such a phrase. He had no desire to express some ineffable, disembodied essence within, to free himself of the inner oppressiveness of selfhood. Neither did the other Greek lyric poets attempt quite this, though it would be at least more truly said in the case of Solon. Werner Jaeger has put this whole point well, writing:

> ...Greek expressions of personal emotion and thought have nothing purely and exclusively subjective in them; it might rather be said that a

shows that we need not consider Archilochus' lampoons products of strong spite: they could have been traditional releases of communal emotion.

poet like Archilochus has learnt how to express in his own personality the whole objective world and its laws – to represent them in himself.[4]

As a poet Archilochus is anxious to register the events of feelings of his own being, rather than to reach to the immovable, and soul-like, in himself. In this he distinguishes himself from the mystic in search of his soul; from the Wordsworth of the *Prelude* as well as from the Symbolist poet – Mallarmé or Verlaine – who is in search of sufficiently attenuated imagery to translate the ineffable in himself. Archilochus relates himself not simply to the far less 'confessional' Hesiod, but to all his fellow Greek lyricists.

The first sense-origin of events for Archilochus is quite naturally his body. If we wish to think of lyric poetry as a step in the discovery of the human being by himself, as part of the *Entdeckung des Menschen*, we cannot be shocked at the quick discovery of the body. A child discovers his body first, and only much later grows aware of the mind inside it. Archilochus is verbally preoccupied by the elements of the life of his body, beginning with its sexual will: preoccupied verbally, that is, as well as in the texture of his meter, which itself often has a transparently erotic rhythm.

A few of his fragments concern his reproductive organs (Fragments 47, 136). To ignore such passages is to make the job of interpreting him more difficult than it already is. Apparently there were few sexual taboos on early Greek poetry, and 'indecency,' as we might call it, was an important ingredient in some deeply religious Greek attitudes. In any case, animal passion ran like electricity through Archilochus' body. He translates it through such lines as (fragment 72):

> Just to fall upon her swelling womb
> Meeting her thigh to thigh.

To make poetry of bluntly physical language is one of his accomplishments, though it is difficult to see this in translation, and that accomplishment is proof enough that Archilochus was in firm artistic control of his 'real' emotions. He could also translate tenderness with the strange, tangible, untranslatable line (fragment 71):

> If only I could touch my loved-one's hand.

A light sensual excitement crosses the line, and leaves it in simple finality. In these lines in which the basic sense-life of the body is

4. Jaeger, *op. cit.*, p. 114.

brought into poetry — scarce lines as everything connected with Archilochus is scarce[5] — we can make out the controlled closeness of that poetry to the poet's sense-life. His sense-life — so very different from that of Homer or Hesiod — is providing the raw material of his poetry.

The *personae* of his body — for to some poets the inner organs become virtually that — sometimes emerge metaphorically as well as literally into Archilochus' poetry. The following lines (fragment 103) are an example:

> Such is the passion for love that has twisted its way beneath my heart-
> strings
> and closed deep mist across my eyes
> stealing the soft heart from inside my body. . .

> (Trans. by Richmond Lattimore)

On the surface we are reminded of the formulaic death of an Homeric hero. The physical picture looks like that. In fact, though, here is an originally worked expression of unusual sense-experience. (Archilochus never disappoints us with facile language). *Kardien* (heart) seems to be meant half-physically, half-symbolically. So do *achlyn* (mist), *stetheon* (heart, midriff), and *phrenas* (mind, heart). We are not yet in the language world — of romantic 'heart,' 'bosom' and 'hand' — which tends to translate the physical into purely non-physical terms. Such niceties were absent from early Greek poetry. Nor do the physical terms in this passage refer to anything merely physical. Archilochus is clearly not considering the same heart a physician considers.

A similarly intermediate physical-spiritual inner event is translated in the following lines (fragment 84):

> Wretchedly I lie desiring,
> Soulless, with an anguish from the gods
> Transfixed, clear through the bones.

The last words, 'transfixed (or struck) through the bones,' are more than a conventional, sentimental lover's outcry, although they are partly that. They seem to translate a physical experience which never

---

5. But constantly less scarce. There have been numerous discoveries, in recent years, which have added both to our knowledge about Archilochus' life, and to the body of his poetry. For a recent survey of additions, cf. A. Giannini, "Archiloco alla luce dei nuovi ritrovamenti," *Acme* 11 (1958) 41 -96.

'really' happened, yet which could not be described in any but physical terms. We assume that Archilochus is dealing with his sense-experience directly, and with great fidelity to its contours. How could he have come, by literary conceit, on this subtly sensuous event?

The chief source of sense-experience for Archilochus, as for most poets, is neither his inner sexual tensions, nor his spiritual-physical romantic feelings. It is the events of his eye. He treats us in his language to many fresh visual experiences. In one of his fine iambs he gives us a pure vision of the eye, undisturbed by reflection (fragment 29):

> She held a branch of myrtle and
> Flowering rose and down her back
> And shoulders flowed her hair.

Fidelity to sense-experience, it seems again, is the source of the poem's purity and stillness. The piece has a pellucid, sensuous surface, which reminds us of some of Archilochus' most erotic fragments (47, 72, 136). That is not to say, in this case or in any of those previously considered, that his verse is a passive 'imitation' of inner events. A poet's symbolical translation of his experience is oblique. Yet we can feel certain that some limpid visual image or images generated this small poem. The border between art and life grows distinct though narrow.

Yet even for Archilochus the eye could not be often merely a passive part of the body. In him, visual awareness tended toward mental awareness, just as the most 'unrefined' bodily awareness did. In the following fragment (fragment 21) we can see comment appended to vision, and emerging from it:

> Like the spine of an ass this island
> Stands, with timber for a crown.
> Not a lovely or a wanted place,
> Or charmed, as one upon the banks of Siris.

Unlike the vision of the last fragment, this one — the first two lines, that is — contains an image, a simile, and in that sacrifices something of its purely visual sense-character. But this vision is not permitted to stand alone. It is merged into an evaluation which it, itself, seemed to point toward. With the addition of a second pair of lines, the mood of the first two is transformed.

The fusion of vision with reflection, their simultaneous expression, is rare in Archilochus, who is so fundamentally a poet of the senses. That is one way of explaining what is unusual in the following often-discussed fragment (58):

> I don't like the towering captain with the spraddly length of leg,
> one who swaggers in his lovelocks and cleanshaves beneath the chin.
> Give me a man short and squarely set upon his legs, a man
> full of heart, not to be shaken from the place he plants his feet.

(Trans. by Lattimore)

The sensual images of the two kinds of men described contain the relevant reasons for their being 'likeable' or not. The participles and adjectives describing the men, through which they are made visible, are also vehicles of Archilochus' attitude toward them. This kind of translation of half-sensuous experience bears some resemblance to the kind of metaphorical language mentioned above (fragments 103,84). It is the language of sense-experience penetrated with attitude and understanding.

In these characteristic ways in which Archilochus uses his visual experience, we can see three stages of the lyric translation of sense-experience; three stages in the formation of the peculiar existential demand made by ancient lyric. The gradual stages of intellectualizing the eye are not only new ranges of Archilochus' poetic power. but they are refinements on the pure receptivity of sense-experience. Yet he never moves very far in the direction of such refinements. In the same way the translation of pure sexual awareness is rare. The body's life needs constantly to be caught up in thought, released and lightened with metaphor. Poetry, or for that matter language itself, is already a decisive step in this kind of release. On the whole, though, Archilochus is distinctive among Greek poets for the patience with which he tries to translate the elementary modes of bodily existence into poetry.

It remains, in this line of discussing Archilochus, to ask whether there are conceptual overtones to his verse. Has he a poetic philosophy? We have seen that he had a point of view, an angle of vision. It emerged more or less directly from his sense-experience. It was not a consistent angle of vision, and not a reflective one: it was the mood in which the outer world happened to occur aesthetically to his senses. Yet there are persistent conceptual overtones in his poetry, and if we had all he wrote we might find these overtones harmonized. As it is, many of his 'ideas' seem to be simply reflexes from his sense-experience. He writes (fragment 65):

> One main thing I understand,
> to come back with deadly evil at the man who does me wrong.
>
> (Trans. by Lattimore)

This 'idea' in Archilochus is hardly more than a stubborn animal reflex, and it recurs often in his poetry. On a more reflective level he offers little except prudent statements based on his direct experience of the world. We read (fragment 66):

> To the god all things are easy. Many times from circumstance
> of disaster they set upright those who have been sprawled at length
> on the ground, but often again when men stand planted on firm feet,
> these same gods will knock them on their backs, and then the evils come,
> so that a man wanders homeless, destitute, at his wit's end.
>
> (Trans. by Lattimore).

These lines mark the minimal effort of an alert person to gain some philosophic control over his destiny. They are lines of folk-wisdom, at most the outcome of experience of life. From his experience he draws a private rule of life (fragment 66):

> . . .and if you beat them, do not brag in open show,
> nor, if they beat you, run home and lie down on your bed and cry.
> Keep some measure in the joy you take in luck, and the degree
> you give way to sorrow. All our life is up-and-down like this.
>
> (Trans. by Lattimore)

Even the tough soldier, who in another fragment insisted that pleasure could make nothing worse, accepts here the wisdom of not tempting fickle gods with displays of extreme feeling. Philosophy was foreign to Archilochus, and could turn him from a vital sense-being into a prudent moralist, out of character. It could carry him, and his genre, back in the direction of Hesiod.

ii

Do we find in Archilochus, as it is often claimed for the Greek lyric poets in general, that he introduces a new awareness of the self, an expression of greater subjectivity after the impersonal age of the Homeric epic? After the rather schizophrenic verbal world of Hesiod, torn between its epic form and its almost lyric demand for personal intervention? The answer is 'yes'; but it needs to be qualified. Certainly the ego is prominent in Archilochus' poetry. He tells us what he feels, what he sees, what he thinks he should do. He represents 'his own' inner life openly, and with ease. In this sense he is conpicuously different from Hesiod, the first European poet to name himself in his work (Homer having refused). When Hesiod tells us that the Muses of Helikon addressed him or that he once travelled to Chalkis in order to participate in a singing-contest, he introduces himself awkwardly. He is not accustomed to 'being in' his poetry. We have discussed this awkwardness. Archilochus is perfectly at ease in his own poetic illusion, benefitting from the happy support provided by his genre; and in turn provided to that genre, by such growing senses of individual ease.

Yet if Archilochus handles himself successfully, as poetic object, he implicitly looks on himself as closely related to the outer world. In this he resembles Solon and Sappho. His best poetry emerges from the point of contact between sense-impressions and his self. This is the secret of his success. Archilochus is only incidentally concerned with the self in a metaphysical sense. He is not plumbing his own depths. Perhaps we should rather say — as Jaeger put it above — that Archilochus is only interested in himself as a subject, and that his poetic stance is one of relative subjectivity.

What, at a closer look, seems to be character of this subjectivity? The double meaning of the word 'subject' may be a clue. Not only does Archilochus appear in his poetry as a grammatical subject, as the subject of various sense-experiences, the person who has those experiences. He appears also in *subjection to* those experiences. This is the more important aspect of his poetic being, an aspect which deserves more attention. Archilochus is a center of awareness which is impinged on by the multitude of sense-impressions which compose the basic level of his world. To this extent he is virtually the victim of his sense-impressions. Sense-impressions are accidents of Archilochus' substance. An historical comment may help to put this subjective situation into a wider context.

In modern times many thinkers — for instance Goethe, Schiller and Kant — have analyzed the aspects of man's being through which he is sensuously aware, that is, the sensuous aspects of his perceptual equipment. Each of those three thinkers found a way to assert that mankind, through its senses, is a part of nature. The sensuous part of the human being is anti-rational, essentially without intelligible form. This part of our natures, they held, is fate, weight, matter. It is true that all three of these thinkers also insisted that man has supra-sensuous powers. Reason (*Vernunft*), in various meanings of the word, was the power they most admired. But sense-experience is cut off from reason. This description and 'location' of sense-experience helps toward understanding the subjectivity of Archilochus – and of Sappho – in its second, passive meaning. A good part of Archilochus' style of being did belong to nature.

There is another relevant historical point here, one made especially strongly by Kant in his reflections on the relation of art to sensuous experience. He argued that aesthetic creativity is one way in which mere sensuous experience can be removed from the realm of nature toward, though never quite to, the realm of Reason. Through form, Kant believed, man can virtually rescue, that is universalize, certain of his fleeting sense-experiences. Kant was only one of many modern thinkers who considered art an effort to mediate between 'lower' and 'higher' human faculties. But Kant's thought is particularly relevant to the present point. His thinking might help us to locate and understand Archilochus' sense-experience, and also to appreciate the context of Archilochus' rescuing of that experience through form. Archilochus was struggling against mere subjection to the sense-world. In this he was in the major tradition of the Greek lyric. This is the context of his, and the other Greek lyricists,' establishment of existential demand.

Along with Archilochus' subjection to sense-experience went a distinctive and eternal lyrical motive: the urge to conquer the mere particularity of the sense-event, the sensual accident which happens to the self.[6] Essentially the self is hostile to the accidental, to luck. A lyric poet wants to translate the here-and-now limitation of sense-experience into a formal expression, art, which confers some exemption from place and time and thus gives the self power over accidents. Archilochus' disciplined, clear poems prove that this motive was powerful in him. It operated, as we can judge, not to control any ordinary sense-world, but to control the particularly intense world of his own senses. That was the world which he struggled to universalize.

---

6. Hermann Fränkel, *Dichtung und Philosophie des frühen Griechentums* (New York, 1951) 191, writes of Archilochus: 'Die Weltgeschichte verblasst gegenüber dem was sich im eignen Umkreis begibt.' Fränkel's whole chapter on Archilochus, pp. 182-207, explores the poetic mentality of the lyric poet ingeniously and from many angles.

Epilogue

Genre and Demand in Greek Literature

Genre and particular kind of pressure or demand have been seen here as complementary notions, and in fact some effort has been made to say that at least in Greek literature these two ideas are inextricably interrelated.

Any effort to support this point is facilitated by the organized developmental procedure of Greek literary history. There is a tidiness in the manner of that self-development, which once more puts us in debt to the clarity with which the Greeks worked out their spiritual history. They seemed to be writing for the convenience of historians.

First came epic. We now know better than before what a complicated, historically involved, up-and-down process the growth of that genus was. The Greek epic was long in the making, entertained peripheral forms of itself (like the *Batrachomyomachia*), shaded itself off into gradually less grand forms, like those written by Hesiod: yet the epic seemingly remained intact as long as it survived, and true to its peculiar nature, about which I tried to make certain points earlier. Then most remarkably, when the epic had begun to wear itself out it passed rapidly out of existence – for some five centuries – to be sharply and cleanly replaced by Greek lyric poetry.

We may still be wrong on our dates, but it looks as though Hesiod wrote in the later eighth century, and as though his work was the last statement of the early Greek epic world. He was in any case closely followed, as far as we know, by such primal lyric poets as Tyrtaeus and Archilochus. Their primacy wants somewhat to be doubted; they seem to write at an already advanced stage of their genre s development. (The broad outlines of our generic picture, however, seem not to be threatened by such doubts.) With the appearance of those poets the lyric world sets in, a world of which we can say that from 700 to 500 it enjoyed almost incredible dominance over literary production in Greece.

The readiness of Greek genre to cut itself off sharply at the extremities is again shown in the clarity with which the lyric yielded, in the late sixth century, to drama and — shortly after — to the beginnings of prose. Here the break seems a little more jagged than that which divided epic from lyric. We know, shadowily, that rustic festivals had already in the sixth century been leading toward tragedy and comedy. And we know that the lyric, in an extended sense, continued elements of its life both in Pindar and in choral passages of Greek tragedy. But by 500 the lyric was, on the whole, part of the past, and drama ruled Athens. Alcman would have been as anomalous in fifth century Athens as Pindar in sixth century Lesbos.

The relative clarity of this temporal sequence helps us to see the relative clarity of the succession of demands made by ancient Greek literature.

I have tried not to over-formulate the character of those demands, to make it seem too distinct, in the various genres. I wanted to let that demand show itself gradually through the argument, and with sufficient flexibility. It is useless to establish a doctrine of genres. Still I think an unmistakeable impression emerges, from a study of Greek literature by kinds, that it can be appropriately organized along the lines of three demands or pressures. And in history these demands did, as it happened, follow a clear order.

It was in the nature of early epic 'material,' and especially of the way Homer treated it, that it should be presented 'objectively.' I have tried to define what the 'objective' means here. It proved to be, in Homer, that which coerces the reader as far as possible by its own concrete firmness, which draws the reader (or hearer) out to it. Art — in the quarrel of itself with didacticism — would in Hesiod be that which most draws the reader out to it, and to the 'natural law' for which it speaks; while in Homer the field of coercion is the self-sufficient world of epic action, value and motive, which one must go out into as into some historical statement.

In Greek lyric, plainly, the kind of demand would be entirely different; even when, as occasionally in Alcman or Theognis, epic-mythical material is embodied. Solon, Sappho, and Archilochus ask us to take an interest in themselves, as makers within their poems. They do not care that we admire their uniqueness, and in fact seem glad to appear as foci, points at which the 'outer world' and the soul meet. But with them these points, at the most outerly, should demand our attention.

The tragedians' demand is the hardest to determine, though its distinctive force begins to be felt, even through the limited kinds of examples taken up in this book. Enough was said earlier to suggest that character and action, in Greek tragedy, are seen through into the centers of personages in literature. The fictitious personage we call Oedipus or Agamemnon or Prometheus or Neoptolemus is in Greek tragedy shaped into a fabric of deep and inwardly perceptions, of felt dilemmas, depths of self-awareness, of powers for transcendence. The 'putting into action' of such characters, as I tried to show in discussing the 'knowing' of Greek tragedy, seems in no way to flatten or superficialize their depth. Rather action here — as is not the case in Greek epic — stimulates and elicits from us increasingly deep levels of response. All this suggests, I suppose, greater kinship of Greek tragedy with Greek lyric than with Homeric epic.

That epic contents itself with what, by contrast to tragedy, seems 'objective presentation.' Seeing just where tragedy's presentation differs from that of lyric is somewhat harder.

It is difficult because it involves stating the obvious in a way that gives insight. A stageful of interacting bodies is different from the syntactical field of force of a lyric poem. Both kinds of presentation, I think, radiate from their makers as center; but in the play diffusion has taken place to a much greater extent. In part the actors take over; in part the scene-makers, the musicians, the mask-makers. Then there are the physical demands of staging. Finally there is simply the question of the fragmentation of the original perception (or mood, or cares) out into a multiplicity of vehicles. The tragedian can, and must, demand attention to this new world of psycho-physical selves; but he must allow us to think it worldlike, inwardly *and* outwardly, part of a vast tale in which, in one sense, the author's self can play no part.

The differences among these three genre-demands are in themselves inexhaustibly meaningful. We see the problems, which they raise, at the center of abstract modern critical concerns — say in the critical assumptions dominant in the thought world of Emil Staiger or Northrup Frye. But in the study of ancient Greek literature, where these differences and their problems are raised in a pristine historical appearance, almost in a literary-historical revelation, the historical factor seems necessarily to want inclusion in the field of literary analysis. We find ourselves up against the barest kind of question: is it important that the three genres developed, in Greece, in the historical order in which they developed, in the order of epic, lyric, tragedy?

This question is as hard as any which touches on 'meaning in history,' and it is essential to answer it in limited terms, to finesse the question of providence. Far this side of that question we can notice, with surprise bordering on wonder, that Greek cultural history 'advances' in a startingly clear sequence of jumps, or stages. This is clear politically, at least in Athens in the passage from feudalism to fifth-century democracy. And it is clear in other arts than literature: in architecture, sculpture, and vase painting, with their astoundingly clean-cut levels of movement, judging from which we find ourselves able, in many cases, to assign particular artifacts to their correct decades, and to see our assignments verified. The stages are this clear on the literary front.

Can each of the three dominant genres be taken as appropriate to the kind of culture from which in fact it was produced? In a sense, yes, but we have to be careful about this kind of assumption. Because feudal societies frequently sponsor epics, and relatively urban, bourgeois societies frequently produce dramas, we can't assume that this state of affairs needs to be so, or that its being so, in a particular case or many cases, can help explain the order of the cases themselves. The argument from the contemporary scenes will only broaden, not deepen, the argument. It will still leave the questions of the importance of the particular historical order untouched.

Some inner logic to the sequence of literary events may take us farther, while at the same time including 'social background' as potential for explanation. Like a Phoenix, Greek literature seems to have reproduced itself, genus by genus, out of its own ashes. The importance of this movement will be seen in some 'meaningfulness' interior to this regenerative process.

The epic demand, in Greek literature, exists as the possibility of a demand other than itself Its coercion into an 'objective' world of action and experience, is a coercion into happened-on meanings, like Achilles' self-mastery at the end of the *Iliad,* like Odysseus' departure from Calypso, which ultimately strain and destroy the assumption of epic production. In Hesiod we see another version of this self-transcending, or self-interiorizing, dynamism in the epic material. In the *Theogony* we see genealogy turning toward a speculative genetic account of man's nature and situation. In the *Works and Days* we see the inherited, highly public material of Farmer's Almanac wisdom inextricably woven into a system of ethics.

The direction of the movement inherent in this genre, is hard to specify; further, that is, than to say that it is a movement 'in,' a spiritual interiorization. There is a 'logic' to this growth in from the center of the oldest genre. Does lyric in any way strike us as the destined heir to epic? Why lyric, not drama?

In answering this question we might, of course, restrict ourselves to the replies offered by political or social history. But there is no reason to suppose that the historical, in *that* sense, would be helpful in any way that the purely literary is not. The genesis of the 'tyrannies' out of the feudal world will only appear inevitable, when it has become accomplished fact.

We can best answer by a kind of shorthand; reminding ourselves that the interiorization of epic, suggested here, is in fact close to the intrusion of an immediate personal voice into the monotone liturgy of the hexameter world. The nearness of this intrusion is felt in Homer, who strangely seems most to approach us when he allows Achilles to return (or desecrate) Hector's body, and most to recede when he offers us opposing battle-lines, moving like scythes. The intrusion appears more obviously, though less compellingly, in Hesiod; when, in a few startling lines, he uses the first-person singular pronoun. The kind of address or pressure, which we here see self exerting through language in Homer and Hesiod, is closer to the direct lyric demand than to the fractured demand of drama. It is not that epic could *not* have produced drama directly; simply that the production of lyric, from epic, *is* internally consequential.

What about the final generic frontier, from lyric to dramatic?

Any account of the internal consequence, here, will have to consider the new complexity of the generating forces, which are now an epic tradition both self-preserved and partially outgiven into the lyric. Tragic drama had both father and mother.

By internal production something essential to epic and something essential to lyric passed into Greek tragedy. What I have called the 'objective' in Greek epic, the impersonally coercive, appears in Greek tragedy, or drama, as the fragmentation of original voice, as the physical properties – whether body, scenery, or bodies in action – which force the spectator to them, and exert little interior pressure. What I have called the demand of the self in Greek lyric persists, in Greek tragedy, as the demand – studied here in *Prometheus Bound* or *Oedipus at Colonus* – that the spectator should match a hero's life with his own life. The double content, and in a sense the superior richness, of Greek tragedy can only be accounted for by such internal, non-historical genetics.

We seem forced to recognize, in considering especially this last generation, that there is an extraordinary comprehensiveness, and fullness, in the entire process by which Greek literature made itself. The components of that development are held to one another, across the lines that distinguish them, by tense harmonic chords, and the whole which they span vibrates like a fulfilled octave.

One trait of that comprehensiveness is that the last element of the generic triad seems to have assumed the first two into itself, and made something new, but oldly new, of them. The essential form of epic and lyric seems to have passed into drama and been remade. That is, there is a kind of total self-realization in the inter-relationship of the members of the generic triad. But that is only part of the point.

Not only do the generic elements, here, interrelate deeply, and fulfill themselves in one another, but in themselves they constitute an astoundingly adequate image of the total demand which literature can make on man, the animal which makes *it*.

Epic makes him go to meet it, on the ground of its inherited outwardliness. Lyric makes him open himself to it, and meet his own image in the recesses. Drama makes him meet his own recesses formed to a compelling outwardliness. Drama is the most complete of the three demands. But the *three demands* taken together stand for man's total power, in language, to rivet and teach his own attention.

INDEX

112

VIZANTYSKY VREMENNIK (Byzantine annals).
Edited by V. G. Valilievsky, V. E. Regel and T. I.
Uspenski. Volume 1-25. St. Petersburg 1894-1928.
Reprint.   Hfl. 3.000,–

EDITIONS RODOPI NV

KEIZERSGRACHT 302-304

AMSTERDAM – THE NETHERLANDS

WAYNE N. THOMPSON

Aristotle's Deduction and Induction:
Introductory Analysis and Synthesis.

Amsterdam 1975. 114 pp.   Hfl. 20,—

Aristotle's logical writings have been highly influential on Western thought, but even in translation these works are lengthy, tiresome and difficult. Moreover, existing commentaries deal more in scholarly argument than in clear, concise exposition.

The principal functions of Mr. Thompson's book are twofold: (1) to present the essential features of Aristotle's logic in a clear, relatively brief form; and (2) to bring together aspects of the system that in the original are widely scattered.

EDITIONS RODOPI NV
KEIZERSGRACHT 302-304
AMSTERDAM – THE NETHERLANDS